ISBN 0-9524823-3-9
©1995 Carlton Publishing and Printing Limited, part of The Carlton Group.
All Rights Reserved.

The Carlton Group
410-420 Rayners Lane
Pinner, Middlesex, HA5 5DY
Telephone: (0181) 429 0056
Facsimile: (0181) 429 3977

Published by: Carlton Publishing and Printing Limited, part of The Carlton Group
The contents of this book are believed correct at the time of printing.
Nevertheless, the publisher can accept no responsibility for errors or omissions or changes
in the details given.

Produced by: Carlton Publishing and Printing Limited and Printed in England.

The World Trade Organisation

and

Gatt'94

—

A

Guide

To The New

International Economic Law

—

by

The Rt Hon. Denzil Davies, MA (Oxford)
Barrister, Former Treasury Minister

Summary

	Page
Chapter 1	3

Chapter 1 is an Introductory Chapter which describes the origins of GATT and explains the background to the Uruguay Round and GATT 1994.

Chapter 2 5

Chapter 2 deals with the structure of the World Trade Organisation.

Chapter 3 7

Chapter 3 deals with the Dispute Settlement Body.

Chapter 4 10

Chapter 4 deals with the main elements of the Agreement on Intellectual Property (TRIPS) including trade in Counterfeit Goods and analyses the application of that Agreement to copyrights, patents and trademarks respectively. The chapter also deals with the very special and novel provisions regarding enforcement of remedies which are laid down in respect of Intellectual Property rights.

Chapter 5 18

Chapter 5 deals with the extension for the first time of GATT to Trade in Services.

Chapter 6 25

Chapter 6 analyses the position of Financial Services, such as Banking and Insurance.

Chapter 7 29

Chapter 7 deals with trade in Industrial Goods.

Chapter 8 32

Chapter 8 deals with Textiles and Clothing including the incorporation of the Multi Fibre Agreement into GATT 1994.

Chapter 9 35

Chapter 9 deals with Agriculture.

Chapter 10 37

Chapter 10 provides three Case Studies in Copyright, Banking and trade in Clothing. These Case Studies provide a guide to private sector bodies as to how they may enforce the remedies, both in private law and public law, which are provided by GATT 1994.

Summary

	Page
Appendix I	45

contains a list of the initial signatories of GATT 1994.

Appendix II 47
reproduces extracts from the Agreement on Intellectual Property Rights (TRIPS).

Appendix III 85
reproduces extracts from the Agreement on Trade in Services.

Appendix IV 98
reproduces the Annex on Financial Services; the Second Annex on Financial Services and the Undertaking on Commitments in Financial Services.

Appendix V 110
lists the Government Libraries where the various Market Access Schedules (see Chapter 5) are available for inspection.

Appendix VI 112
Sets out the Working Procedures of the Dispute Settlement Body.

October 1995

Denzil Davies
8 Gray's Inn Square
Gray's Inn
London, WC1R 5AZ
Tel: (0171) 242 3529
Fax: (0171) 404 0395

Chapter 1

Background

---

1. The Final Act embodying the results of the Uruguay Round of the Multilateral Trade Negotiations ("GATT 1994") was formally signed in Marrakesh, Morocco on 15th April 1994 by 111 participating nations. Another 14 smaller countries will sign later in Geneva. See Appendix 1. GATT 1994 was the culmination of negotiations which commenced in Punta Del Este, Uruguay in September 1986. The one significant omission is China. China was a founder member of GATT but left when the Communists took over. At the time of writing China is negotiating terms with the United States which hopefully will lead to its joining GATT 1994.

2. GATT was originally formed by the Geneva Agreement of 1947 ("GATT 1947"). GATT was established to reduce high tariffs on goods. High tariffs were seen as likely to cause trade wars; trade wars could lead to military wars.

3. GATT 1947 had aimed to establish a new body, the International Trade Organisation to oversee world trade and to provide a framework of rules and obligations. The International Trade Organisation never came into existence. The United States Congress baulked at creating a world trade body which could challenge national sovereignty in matters of international trade.

4. GATT 1947 ended up as a contractual arrangement between its initial members without a rule-making and a rule-enforcing institution. A secretariat continues to live in Geneva. It has been formally known as the International Committee of the International Trade Organisation. GATT 1947 did not have an international legal personality.

---

5. GATT 1994 has substantially fulfilled the original intentions and purposes of GATT 1947. An international rule-making and rule-enforcing body, the World Trade Organisation, see Chapter 2 below, is to be established.

6. GATT 1947 was concerned with trade in goods. GATT 1994 for the first time extends the principles of free trade into other areas, in particular into trade in services and the protection of intellectual property rights. Patents, Trademarks, Copyright etc will now for the first time be subject to the GATT rules.

7. The World Trade Organisation came into force on 1st January 1995

Chapter 2

The World Trade Organisation

1. The Uruguay Round was brought formally to an end by the Final Act signed at Marrakesh, Morocco on 15th April 1994 by 111 states. See Chapter 1 above and Appendix I below.

2. The Final Act recorded, *inter alia*, the agreement of the signatories to the establishment of the World Trade Organisation ("WTO").

3. It is the WTO which effectively gives the force of law to the Uruguay Round. GATT 1947 is incorporated into the WTO framework. The existing countries which are members of GATT will automatically become members of the WTO. The whole of GATT 1947 with the regulations, rules and procedures which have grown up since its inception will be transferred into the WTO.

4. The WTO will provide the institutional framework for the mechanisms set up under the various Uruguay Round Agreements. In particular it provides the framework for the Dispute Settlement Body. See Chapter 3 below.

5. The WTO will be headed by a Ministerial Conference which will meet at least once every two years. A General Council will be established to oversee the operation of the Agreement.

6. The practical work of servicing the agreements will be undertaken by the WTO Secretariat which, headed by a Secretary General, will be based in Geneva and will be drawn from the existing GATT Secretariat.

7. The WTO Agreement provides in Article XVI(4) that each participating Nation shall ensure that its laws, regulations and administrative procedures conform with its obligations under the GATT 94 Agreements. If a participating Nations fails to ensure that its laws, etc are in

conformity with its obligations under the WTO Agreement as mentioned above, then that Nation will either (a) have to bring any domestic law into conformity with the rules of the WTO Agreement; or (b) offer compensatory market access to the Nation which has complained about the failure to conform with the obligations; or (c) to accept the retaliatory withdrawal of market access by the complaining Nation. The compensation and retaliation must be proportionate in value to the impairment of rights or market access opportunities which was caused by the failure to conform.

8. A copy of the WTO Agreement can be obtained from HMSO on reference Misc 15 (1994) Cm 2571.

9. The postal address of the Information Division of the WTO at the date hereof is 154, rue de Lausanne, CH-1211 Geneva 21, Switzerland, and the telephone number is 739 5111.

Chapter 3

Dispute Settlement Body

1. The WTO Agreement sets up a Dispute Settlement Body ("DSB") to resolve disputes between participating Nations.

2. Complaints alleging that a participating Nation is not abiding by its obligations are initially most likely to come from the private sector. Only the government of the participating Nation whose private sector bodies have been adversely affected can initiate proceedings with the WTO against the offending participating Nation and utilise the dispute settlement procedures of the DSB. See Chapter 10 below.

3. Although a complaint to the WTO can only be made by the governmental authorities of a participating Nation, private sector bodies who raise complaints in the first place with their Governments should be aware of the mechanisms of the complaint procedures and the way disputes are resolved by the DSB. A knowledge of the mechanisms will enable the private sector bodies to influence the way in which their Government presents their case and thus influence the eventual outcome. Usually the bodies will have a better knowledge of their own trading activities than the civil servants who will be conducting the complaint.

4. **Complaint procedures**

    (i)   The Nation against which the complaint is made must initially enter into bilateral consultations with the complainant Nation within 30 days of the making of the complaint.

    (ii)   If after 60 days there is no settlement, the complainant Nation may request that the DSB establish a Panel. Where consultations are refused by the Nation against which the complaint is made then the complainant Nation may directly ask for a Panel.

(iii) A Panel will be established unless the DSB decides by consensus against establishing one.

(iv) Panels normally consist of three persons of appropriate background and experience from countries which are not parties to the dispute. The WTO Secretariat will maintain a list of experts satisfying the criteria.

(v) Panel procedures are set out in detail at Article 12 of the Understanding on Dispute Settlements. See Appendix VI below.

(vi) The Panel will normally complete its work and issue a report within 6 months or, in cases of urgency, within 3 months.

(vii) Within 60 days of the issue of the report, the DSB will publish the report and adopt it unless the DSB decides by consensus against doing so.

(viii) The complainant Nation may then notify the DSB of its intention to appeal.

(ix) The appeal will go to the Appellate Body which is established by the WTO Agreement. The Appellate Body is composed of 7 members, 3 of whom will serve on any one case. An appeal is limited to issues of law covered in the Panel report and legal interpretations developed by the Panel. Appellate proceedings must not exceed 60 days from the date a Nation formally notifies its decision to appeal. The resulting report must be adopted by the DSB and unconditionally accepted by the parties within 30 days following its issue unless the DSB decides by consensus against its adoption.

(x) If the country against which the complaint has been made has been found "guilty" then it will be able to chose from one of the three "punishments" mentioned at paragraph 7 of Chapter 2 above.

(xi)   The Nation in whose favour a Panel has reported and which has the right to establish retaliation or seek compensatory market access may do so in trading areas which are different from those that are the subject matter of the dispute. For example, if suitable scope for retaliation does not exist within the trading sector in which the dispute has occurred it will be possible to look to another trading sector. Retaliation against a breach of intellectual property obligations, for example, could take the form of withdrawal by the complainant Nation of tariff concessions on goods. This form of retaliation obviously might not be satisfactory to the private sector bodies which initially raised the complaint since the compensation might not occur in the trading sector in which the private sector bodies are operating. See Chapter 10 below.

Chapter 4

Intellectual Property And Counterfeit Goods ("TRIPS")

1. For the first time GATT will apply to intellectual property rights including trade in counterfeit goods. The Agreement on intellectual property rights ("TRIPS") is published by HMSO, Misc 29 (1994) Cm 2557 and extracts from it are reproduced at Appendix II below.

2. What rights are protected?

A. Copyright

(i) Participating Nations have agreed to comply with the provisions of Articles 1 through 21 of the Berne Convention (1971) and the Appendix thereto for the protection of literary and artistic works. See Article 9(1) at Appendix II below.

(ii) Participating Nations will not be required to protect under GATT moral rights as conferred by article 6 bis of the Berne Convention. See Article 9(1) at Appendix II below.

(iii) Computer programs are protected as literary works under the Berne Convention. See Article 10 at Appendix II below.

(iv) Participating Nations have agreed that data bases should be protected by copyright. To qualify for protection data bases must include a significant intellectual content. See Article 10 at Appendix II below.

(v) The authors of *computer programs* and producers of *sound recordings* are given the right to authorise or to prohibit the commercial rental of their work to the public. A similar exclusive right is given to *films*. The protection must last for 50 years. This means that each participating Nation must provide through its domestic law for such protection both in respect of its nationals

and the nationals of all participating Nations. See Article 14 at Appendix II below.

(vi)   *Broadcasting organisations* may control the use which can be made of broadcast signals. This right lasts for 20 years. See Article 14 at Appendix II below.

B. Trademarks, Industrial Designs And Integrated Circuits

(i)   Participating Nations have agreed that they will adhere to the Paris Convention for the Protection of Industrial Property (1967). See Articles 1, 2 and 3 of Appendix II below.

(ii)   TRIPS defines what is eligible for protection by participating Nations as a *trade or service mark* and what the minimum rights conferred on owners of such marks must be. See Section 2 at Appendix II below.

(iii)   Additional protection is given to trademarks which have been well known in a particular country. See Article 15 at Appendix II below.

(iv)   Participating Nations must ensure that initial registration and each renewal thereof shall be for a term of not less than 7 years. See Article 18 at Appendix II below.

(v)   All participating Nations must provide protection for *industrial designs* for a period of at least 10 years. See Article 26(3) at Appendix II below.

(vi)   With regard to *Layout Designs of Integrated Circuits*, TRIPS requires participating Nations to provide protection on the basis of the Treaty on Intellectual Property in respect of Integrated Circuits adapted at Washington on 26 July 1989 but with the following additional obligations:

– Protection must be available for a minimum period of 10 years;

– the rights must extend to articles incorporating infringing layout designs;

– innocent infringers must be allowed to use or sell stock in hand or ordered before learning of the infringement against a suitable royalty;

– re-licensing and government use is only allowed under a number of strict conditions. See Article 2 and Section 6 at Appendix II below.

C. Patents
(i)　The TRIPS Agreement imposes a general obligation to comply with the substantive provisions of the Paris Convention (1967). See Articles 1, 2 and 3 at Appendix II below.

(ii)　In addition to (i) above TRIPS requires that twenty year patent protection shall be available for all inventions, whether of products or processes in almost all fields of technology. See Article 33 at Appendix II below.

(iii)　Inventions may be excluded from patentability if their commercial exploitation is prohibited for reason of public order or morality. See Article 27(2) at Appendix II below.

(iv)　There are permitted exclusions from the above obligations on patents:

– for diagnostic, therapeutic or surgical methods;

– for plants and animals (other than micro-organisms);

– for essentially biological processes for the production of plants or animals (other than non-biological and micro-biological processes). See Article 27(3) of Appendix II below.

(v)   Plant varieties must be patentable either by patents or by a sui generis system. See Article 27(3)(b) at Appendix II below.

(vi)   Detailed conditions are laid down for compulsory licensing of governmental use of patents without the authorisation of the patent owner. See Article 31 at Appendix II below.

(vii)   Rights conferred in respect of patents for processes must extend to the products directly obtained by the process. See Articles 28 and 34 at Appendix II below.

3. When does TRIPS become enforceable?

(i)   Developed countries are given one year from the establishment of the WTO, on 1st January 1995, to bring their legislation and practices into conformity with the obligations and requirements contained in TRIPS and GATT 1994. See Article 65(1) at Appendix II below.

(ii)   Developing countries and countries which are in the process of transforming from centrally planned economies to market economies are given a five year transition period. See Article 65(2)(3) at Appendix II below.

(iii)   Least developed countries are allowed a transitional period of eleven years. See Article 66 at Appendix II below.

(iv)   In the case of the filing of patents for pharmaceutical and agricultural chemical products in most developed countries special rules in respect of implementation apply. See Article 70 at Appendix II below.

(v)   The general rule is that the obligations contained in TRIPS apply to existing intellectual property rights as well as to new ones. See Article 70 at Appendix II below.

(vi)   To ascertain whether a country falls into one of the special designations at (ii) and (iii) above it is advisable to consult the WTO. See Chapter 2 above.

4. Enforcement of Rights under TRIPS

TRIPS establishes a radical and unique method for the enforcement of intellectual property rights. These enforcement measures go much further than the general measures of enforcement and remedies which are contained in the other provisions of GATT 1994. They place an obligation upon participating Nations to ensure that their domestic law conforms to the obligations created by TRIPS. This means that the GATT obligations contained in TRIPS can become directly enforceable in the domestic courts of participating Nations. The position is somewhat similar to that which occurs in the European Union when directives issued by the European Commission become directly enforceable in the domestic courts of Member States.

(i) Private Law Remedies

(a)   Each participating Nation has entered into a *National-Treatment Commitment.*
       Nationals of other participating Nations must be given treatment in respect of the protection of intellectual property rights which is not less favourable than that which is accorded by participating Nations to their own nationals. See Article 3 at Appendix II below.

(b)   Each participating Nation has also entered into a <u>*Most Favoured Nation*</u> commitment. That means that whatever advantage a participating Nation gives in the field of intellectual property to the nationals of another participating

Nation, it must be extended immediately and unconditionally to the nationals of all other participating Nations, even if such treatment is more favourable than that which the participating Nation gives to its own nationals. See Article 4 at Appendix II below.

(c) *A number of civil, administrative and criminal remedies which must be made enforceable by the domestic nation in its own courts and tribunals are spelled out in TRIPS:-*

- Injunctions and civil damages. See Articles 44 and 45 at Appendix II below.

- A right for judicial authorities to dispose of or destroy goods that infringe intellectual property rights; see Article 46 at Appendix II below.

- Authority to the judicial authorities to order prompt and effective provisional measures in circumstances where any delay is likely to cause irreparable harm to the holder of the intellectual property rights or where evidence is likely to be destroyed. See Article 50 at Appendix II below.

- Judicial review of final administrative decisions; see Article 41(4) at Appendix II below.

- Action for the suspension by Customs authorities of the release into domestic circulation of counterfeit and pirated goods; see Article 51 at Appendix II below.

- The provision of criminal procedures and penalties in cases of wilful trademark, counterfeiting or copyright piracy on a commercial scale. The penalties should include imprisonment and fines which are sufficient to act as a deterrent. See Article 61 at Appendix II below.

(ii) **WTO Remedies** see also Chapters 3 above and 10 below.

The failure by a participating Nation to abide by the commitments described at para 5(i)(a) and (b) above and a failure to provide the domestic remedies described at para 5(i)(c) can also be enforced on a government to government basis through the DSB. See Chapters 1 and 2 above and Chapter 10 below.

5. Practical steps when confronted with a TRIPS copyright "problem".

(i) Determine through normal legal principles which right has been infringed by the offending Nation.

(ii) Ascertain whether the offending Nation is a signatory of GATT 1994 and a member of WTO. See Appendix I below. If the offending Nation is not on the list of initial signatories check with WTO to ascertain whether it signed later. See Chapter 2 above.

(iii) If the offending Nation is a member of WTO, check whether the TRIPS obligations are yet enforceable in respect of that Nation. See para 3(i)(ii)(iii) above.

(iv) If in doubt whether the offending Nation is a developed country or a developing country or a country in the process of transforming from a centrally planned economy to a market economy or a least developed country - see para 3(i)(ii)(iii) above, check with WTO. See Chapter 2 above.

(iv) If the offending Nation is bound by TRIPS, obtain professional advice in the offending Nation as to the chances of seeking redress through the domestic courts of the offending Nation.

(vi)   A wide range of remedies should be available in the domestic courts of the offending Nation. See para 4(i)(c) above and Case Study A at chapter 10 below.

(vii)   If advice from the offending Nation indicates that remedies are available in the domestic courts of that Nation, then instructions can be given to professional advisers in that Nation to proceed that way.

(viii) If remedies are not available in the offending Nation or if, despite the availability of such remedies, it is desired to invoke the WTO remedies, contact the Intellectual Property section of the DTI. Telephone 0171 438 4770.

(ix)   Inform the DTI that it is desired to make a complaint against the offending Nation for failure to comply with TRIPS obligations.

(x)   To make the complaint, follow the procedure set out at Case Study A at chapter 10 below.

Chapter 5

Trade in Services

1. What services are covered

(i) The General Agreement on Trade in Services ("the Services Agreement") provides a new framework of multi-lateral rules to govern trade in services. The Services Agreement covers all services supplied by participating nations which affect trade in services.

(ii) The Services Agreement defines "services" so as to include any service in any sector except services provided in the exercise of governmental authority. See Article 1 at Appendix III below.

(iii) There is a supply of services within the terms of the Services Agreement where:

- services are supplied from the territory of one participating Nation to the territory of another;

- services are supplied from the territory of one participating Nation to the consumers of any other participating Nation *(for example tourism);*

- services are provided through the presence of services-providing entities of one participating Nation in the territory of another *(for example banking);*

- services are provided by nationals of one participating Nation in the territory of any other *(for example construction projects or consultancies).* See Article I at Appendix III below.

(iv)   The Services Agreement is a general agreement covering all services. There are, however, contained in Annexes and Schedules numerous exceptions, exemptions and modifications to the Services Agreement. These exceptions vary in content and scope from nation to nation and from service sector to service sector.

(v)   The most important Annexes relate to;

  – the movement of persons;
  – air transport services;
  – financial services;
  – maritime transport services;
  – telecommunications.

For Financial Services the reader is referred to Chapter 6 below.

For the above annexes the reader is referred to the General Agreement on Trade in Services with Annexes. HMSO Misc. No.28 (1994) 2556.

Appendix III below sets out extracts from the Services Agreement; and Appendix IV below lists the Libraries where the Market Access Schedules (see para 2(iii) below) can be found.

2. What obligations are imposed upon participating Nations?

The Services Agreement imposes upon participating Nations three basic obligations: a *Most-Favoured Nation obligation;* a *Transparency obligation;* and a *Market Access* obligation.

(i)   Most Favoured Nation Obligation

Each participating Nation must accord immediately and unconditionally to the services and service providers of any other participating Nation treatment which is no less favourable than that which it accords to like services and service providers of any other participating Nation. See Article II at Annex III below. However, the agreement does recognise that Most-Favoured-Nation treatment may not be possible for every service activity and therefore it is envisaged that participating Nations may indicate specific exemptions to this obligation. Conditions for such an exemption are included as an annex and they provide for reviews after five years and a normal limitation of 10 years on their duration. See Annex on Article II Exemptions at Appendix III below.

(ii)   Transparency Obligation
This obligation requires the publication by each participating Nation of all the relevant laws and regulations which domestically apply to trade in services. See Article III at Appendix III below. Since domestic regulations, rather than border measures provide the more significant influence on trade in services, the provisions spell out that all domestic measures of general application should be administered in a reasonable, objective and impartial manner. There is a requirement that participating nations must establish the means for prompt review of administrative decisions relating to the supply of services.

(iii)   Market Access Obligation
Participating Nations have agreed that they will publish Schedules covering specific Service sectors where they will bind themselves to give any other participating Nation treatment which is not less favourable than that provided for their own nationals as set out in the conditions and limitations contained in the Schedules published by the participating Nation.

These Schedules in general will embody the restrictions which each domestic nation maintains at present. These restrictions are then "bound" under the Services Agreement so that in effect the domestic nation gives a guarantee to services exporters of other participating Nations that the restrictions will not be subsequently tightened.

To discover what the legal position is at any particular time in respect of trade in services the professional adviser should consult not only the general published obligations of each domestic participating nation under the Transparency Obligations but also the Market Access schedules relating to particular service sectors. All the Market Access Schedules should be available at the Libraries listed at Appendix V below.

(iv)   The Services Agreement also establishes the basis for the progressive liberalisation in the service area through successive rounds of negotiations and the development of national schedules.

It also permits after a period of three years parties to withdraw or modify commitments made in their Market Access Schedules. Where commitments are modified or withdrawn negotiations should be undertaken with interested parties to agree on compensatory adjustments. Where agreement cannot be reached compensation will be decided by arbitration. See Article XXI at Appendix III below.

3. When are the obligations enforceable?

(i)   The Services Agreement is part of GATT 1994 and so its implementation will take place at the same time as the whole of GATT 1994 is implemented and the WTO is set up. See Chapter 1 and Chapter 2 above.

(ii)   However, in view of the complexities of the Services Agreement, especially the annexes and Market Access Schedules, it would be imprudent to assume that all the obligations in respect of trade in services arise immediately the WTO is established. It is advisable, therefore, to check with the Services section of the Department of

Trade and Industry as to whether obligations are already in force in relation to a particular service or service sector. The relevant DTI telephone number is (0171) 215 6167.

4. Enforcement of Rights

(i) Private law remedies

(a) The Services Agreement contains a number of provisions whereby a national of a foreign participating Nation must be provided with judicial, arbitral or administrative procedures to enable a national of a foreign participating Nation to protect its rights under the Services Agreement in the domestic participating Nation. See Article VI at Appendix III below; also Chapter 10 below.

(b) It should be appreciated that the scope for using private law remedies in the offending participating Nation are more limited than they are in the case of the TRIPS agreement. See para 4(i) of Chapter 4 above. A private sector body therefore is more likely to have to seek redress thought the remedies established in the framework of the WTO.

(ii) WTO remedies

(a) Three obligations are placed upon a participating Nation by the Services Agreement; that is the Most-Favoured Nation obligation; the Transparency obligation; and the Market Access obligation. See para 2 above.

(b) A framework for enforcing the above obligations is provided by the WTO and the DSB. See chapters 2 and 3 above.

(c) Guidance as to how a private sector body can utilise the remedies provided by the WTO is provided at para 5 below and at Case Study B in chapter 10 below.

5. Practical Steps when confronted with a Services "problem."

(i)   Obtain from the offending participating Nation information regarding the laws etc which are in force regarding trade in services as required by the Transparency Obligation. A participating Nation must establish enquiry points for the provision of such information. See Article III of the Services Agreement at Appendix III below.

(ii)   If the information requested as at (i) above is not forthcoming, ask the DTI to supply the information. The relevant telephone number is 0171 215 6167.

(iii)   Check whether the offending participating Nation has published Market Access Schedules with regards to the particular service with respect to which there is an alleged transgression. See Appendix IV below.

(iv)   Check whether the Services Agreement has been modified in respect to the particular service by a specific Annex. See para 1(iv)(v) above. Also consult the General Agreement on Trade in Services with Annexes; HMSO MISC No. 28 (1994).

(v)   After consulting the Services Agreement with Annexes; the information provided by the offending participating Nation under the Transparency Obligation; and the Market Access Schedules, identify the specific and particular area of complaint and alleged transgression.

(vi)   Obtain professional advice from within the offending participating Nation as to whether the domestic law of that Nation would provide a remedy for the alleged transgression. See Article VI of the Services Agreement at Appendix III below.

(vii) If the advice from the offending participating Nation indicates that remedies are available in the courts of that Nation, then instructions can be given to professional advisers in the offending Nation to proceed that way.

(viii) If remedies are not available in the offending participating Nation or if, despite the availability of such remedies, it is desired to invoke the WTO remedies and make a complaint, contact the Services section of the DTI. The relevant telephone number is (0171) 215 6167.

(ix) Inform the DTI that it is desired to make a complaint against the offending participating Nation for failure to comply with the Services Agreement.

(x) To make the complaint, follow the procedures set out at Case Study B at chapter 10 below.

Chapter 6

Financial Services

1. What are Financial Services?

Financial Services are defined and described in the Annex on Financial Services. See Appendix IV below. A financial service is any service of a financial nature which is carried out by a financial services supplier of a participating Nation. Financial services include all insurance and insurance related services and all banking and other financial services.

2. What obligations are imposed on Trade in Financial Services?

(i) Trade in Financial Services is governed by the general rules and obligations which are set out in the Services Agreement. See Chapter 5 above.

(ii) However, the Services Agreement is modified in respect of trade in Financial Services by the Second Annex on Financial Services and by the Understanding on Commitments in Financial Services. See Appendix IV below.

(iii) The Second Annex on Financial Services limits, in respect of Financial Services the obligations which are generally imposed upon participating Nations by the Services Agreement. See chapter 5 above. This is done in two ways.

(iv) First, the Second Annex limits the obligations of participating Nations to apply Most-Favoured Nation status to trade in services (see (para 2(i) of chapter 5 above).

A participating Nation may list measures relating to financial services which limit the Most-Favoured Nation obligation, provided that the participating Nation does so in a period of 60 days beginning four months after the date of the establishment of the WTO.

If a participating Nation does not avail itself of this opportunity within the time period then the Services Agreement applies in full and the Most-Favoured Nation obligation is applicable to trade in Financial Services in the same way as trade in other services. See the Second Annex on Financial Services at Appendix IV below; see also the Understanding on Commitments in Financial Services at Appendix IV below.

(v) The second limitation contained in the Second Annex is concerned with the Market Access Schedules which each participating Nation has to publish in respect of trade in services as laid down in the Services Agreement. See para 2(iii) of chapter 5 above

Article 2 of the Second Annex allows a participating Nation a period of 60 days, beginning four months after the date of entry into force of the WTO, to improve, modify or withdraw all or part of any specific commitments on financial services which are contained in its Market Access Schedule. See Appendix IV below. If the participating Nation avails itself of this provision then it can limit, or indeed improve, its commitments on financial services. If it does not avail itself of the provision within the time limit, then the normal rules which govern trade in services as laid down by the Services Agreement also apply to financial services. See Chapter 5 above and the Understanding on Commitments in Financial Services at Appendix IV below.

3. When are the obligations enforceable?

Subject to the special provisions mentioned at paragraph 1 above in relation to trade in Financial Services, the implementation of the provisions on Financial Services will follow the general provisions contained in the Services Agreement. See para 3 of chapter 5 above.

4. Enforcement of rights

The enforcement procedures and remedies in respect of trade in Financial Services are similar to those in the case of all trade in services as laid down by the Services Agreement. See para 4 at Chapter 5 above and Chapter 10 below.

5. Practical steps when confronted with a Financial Services "problem".

(i)   Obtain from the offending participating Nation information regarding the laws etc in force with respect to trade in financial services as required by the Transparency Obligation. A participating Nation must establish enquiry points for the provision of such information. See Article III of the Services Agreement at Appendix III below.

(ii)   If the information requested as at (i) above is not forthcoming, ask the DTI to supply the information. The relevant telephone number is (0171) 215 6167.

(iii)   Check whether the offending participating Nation has published Market Access Schedules in relation to financial services. See Appendix IV below.

(iv)   Check whether the Services Agreement has been modified in respect of financial services by the offending Nation through a specific Annex. See para 1(iv)(v) at chapter 5 above. Also consult the General Agreement on Trade in Services with Annexes. HMSO MISC No. 28 (1994).

(v)   Check whether the offending participating Nation has limited its obligations to apply the Most Favoured Nation status to financial services. See para 1(iv) above. This information should be available at the Services section of the DTI. The relevant telephone number is (0171) 215 6167.

(vi)   Check whether the offending participating Nation has limited in respect of trade in financial services its Market Access Schedules. See para 1(v) above. It is best to check with the Services section of the DTI for this information. The relevant telephone number is (0171) 215 6167.

(vii) After consulting the Services Agreement with Annexes; the information provided by the offending Participating Nation under the Transparency obligation; the Market Access Schedules; the DTI as to whether the offending participating Nation has modified its financial services obligation; then identify the particular financial service in respect of which the alleged transgression has been committed.

(viii) Obtain professional advice from within the offending participating Nation as to whether the domestic law will provide a remedy for the alleged transgression. See Article VI of the Services Agreement at Appendix III below.

(ix) If advice from the offending participating Nation indicates that remedies are available in the domestic courts of that Nation, then instructions can be given to professional advisers in that Nation to proceed that way.

(x) If remedies are not available in the offending Nation or if, despite the availability of such remedies, it is desired to invoke the WTO remedies, contact the Services section of the DTI. The relevant telephone number is (0171) 215 6167.

(xi) Inform the DTI that it is desired to make a complaint against the offending participating Nation for failing to comply with the financial services aspect of the services Agreement.

(xii) To make the complaint, follow the procedures set out at Case Study B at chapter 10 below.

Chapter 7

Industrial Goods

---

1. Market Access

(i)   Lowering tariffs on industrial goods was the main purpose of GATT when it was founded in 1947 and has been the central element of all the GATT regulations. When GATT was founded the average tariff levels in the industrial countries stood at around 40 per cent. At the time of the commencement of the Uruguay Round in 1986 the tariffs of developed countries on industrial goods averaged 5 per cent, although this covered a very wide range of duties extending from zero to over 50 per cent.

(ii)   Tariff reductions agreed by the European Union on behalf of its member states under GATT 1994 average 37 per cent on industrial goods. The value of the average tariff cuts made by the United States, Japan and Canada on all imports of industrial goods from the member states of the European Union will be approximately 50 per cent on a trade weighted basis.

(iii)   Schedules which are deposited by each participating nation with the World Trade Organisation will set out the reductions in tariffs to be made by each country for specific individual goods. The Schedules are very detailed. There is one schedule which amourts to 550 pages which covers all the member nations of countries in the European Union. Appendix V contains information as to how to obtain copies of all the respective schedules.

(iv)   The Uruguay Round Agreements on Trade in Industrial Goods can be obtained from HMSO under the following references: Misc No. 16 (1994) 2558; Misc No. 21 (1994) 2566; Misc No. 22 (1994) 2567.

---

2. Implementation

(i) Tariff reductions will start to take effect from 1st January 1995 when the WTO became established.

(ii) In the European Union, the European Commission has now prepared a draft Council Decision which accepts the WTO Agreement. This will require the assent of the European Parliament but no changes to primary legislation within the United Kingdom are expected to be necessary.

(iii) For most industrial goods the tariff reductions agreed upon by each participating nation shall be implemented in five equal rate reductions, except as may be otherwise specified in the participating Nation's Schedule. The first such reduction shall be made effective on the date of entry into force of the Agreement Establishing the WTO. Each successive reduction shall be made effective on 1st January of each of the following years, and the final rate shall become effective no later than the date four years after the date of entry into force of the Agreement Establishing the WTO. However, participating Nations may implement reductions in fewer stages if they so wish.

(iv) As stated at para 2(iii) above, most tariff reductions on industrial goods will generally be phased over five years. Pharmaceuticals, however, will be tariff-free on the implementation date. Tariffs on beer will be reduced over a period of eight years and in the case of some chemicals and of paper, steel and textiles there will be a period of 12 years before the tariffs are totally eliminated.

3. Enforcement and remedies

(i) GATT 1994, like GATT 1947, is an agreement between nation states. The primary interest in enforcing the agreements on tariff reductions lies with the participating Nations notwithstanding that private sector businesses are directly affected if countries to which they export fail to honour their obligations and to reduce the tariffs in accordance with GATT 1994.

(ii)   GATT 1994 has, however, considerably strengthened the institutional framework for enforcement and for the provision of remedies. These are now to be governed by the WTO and also by the Agreement on Dispute Settlements which establishes the Dispute Settlement Body (DSB). See Chapters 2 and 3 above and Case Study C at chapter 10 below.

Chapter 8

Textiles And Clothing

1. Much of the trade in textiles and clothing has for over 30 years been governed by the Multi Fibre Arrangement (MFA).

2. The MFA involves internationally sanctioned bilateral deals made between nation states. These deals usually contain a mixture of both tariffs and quotas.

3. GATT 1994 incorporates the MFA into GATT over a 10 year period. The period is intended to commence when the WTO is set up.

4. The Agreement on Textiles and Clothing which provides for the incorporation can be obtained from HMSO on reference Misc No. 18 (1994) Cm 2561.

5. Incorporation of MFA into GATT 1994

(i) The phasing out of the MFA and its incorporation into GATT 1994 will take place in four stages.

(ii) The phase out will be calculated according to 1990 trade levels. Each participating Nation which wishes to maintain some quotas will have to examine its 1990 trade and eliminate any quotas on a proportion of products over a 10 year period.

(iii) In Year 1, that is the year of the entry into force of GATT 94, at least 16 per cent of a participating Nation's total imports in four categories of textile and clothing, namely tops and yarns; fabrics; made-up textile products; and clothing are to be eliminated. As explained at para. 5 (ii) above 1990 is treated as the base year for this purpose. On products where quotas have not been eliminated levels of quota are to be increased annually by not less than the growth rate specified in the MFA, increased by 16 per cent. This increase in quotas on imports "left in" the MFA reflects the desire of nations, in particular the United States, that the MFA should "grow out" at the same time as its incorporation is taking place into the GATT.

(iv)   In Year 4 a further 17 per cent of total trade (with 1990 as the base year) is to be incorporated into GATT 1994 and any quota restrictions in force on these products are to be eliminated. On products where quotas remain, "growing out" is to be achieved (see para. 5 (iii) above) by increasing annually the level of quotas on these products by the growth rate specified in MFA plus 25 per cent.

(v)   In year 7 a further 18 per cent of trade will be returned to normal GATT rules and any quota restrictions in force on the products covered will be eliminated. On products where quotas remain, the level of a quota will be increased annually by the growth rate specified in the MFA increased by 27 per cent.

(vi)   In Year 10 all the remaining quotas will be abolished.

6. Enforcement and remedies

(i)   A Textile Monitoring Body (TMB) will be created to supervise the phase out of the MFA. It will have the authority to make recommendations and observations and to resolve disputes. The TMB will submit a comprehensive report on the implementation of each stage of the phase out. Representations will have to be submitted at least 5 months before the end of each stage. These reports may also include recommendations for future action.

(ii)   The Agreement also contains a specific transitional safeguard mechanism which can be applied to products which have not at any stage been incorporated into GATT. Action under this mechanism can be taken against individual exporting countries if it were demonstrated by the importing country that overall imports of a product were entering the country in such increase of quantities as to cause or thereafter cause serious damage, or to threaten it, to the relevant domestic industry and that there was a sharp and substantial increase of imports from the individual country concerned.

(iii)   Action under the safeguard mechanism can be taken either by mutual agreement, following consultations, or unilaterally. Any such action, however, is subject to review by the TMB. If action is taken the level of restraint should be fixed at a level not lower than the actual level of exports or imports from the country concerned during the 12 month period ending 2 months before the month in which a request for consultation was made. Safeguard restraints could remain in place for up to 3 years without extension or until the product is removed from the scope of the agreement, that is integrated into the GATT, whichever comes first.

(iv)   The Agreement on Textiles and Clothing includes provisions to cope with possible circumvention of commitments through transshipment, re-routing, false declaration concerning country or place of origin and falsification of official documents.

(v)   Once a percentage of textiles and clothing imports has left the MFA and has been incorporated into GATT then the enforcement rules and remedies which apply in general under GATT 1994 will be applicable. See Chapters 2 and 3 above and Case Study C at chapter 10 below.

Chapter 9

Agriculture

1. The Agreement on Agriculture covers three distinct areas; market access for agricultural products, domestic support provided by governments for agriculture and export subsidies.

2. Domestic support and export subsidies are matters which are outside the scope of this work.

3. Market access provisions however can be of importance to private businesses in the United Kingdom who export or import agricultural products. Accordingly, the Agreement on Agriculture as it relates to market access is analysed below. Copies of the Agreement can be obtained from HMSO on reference, Misc No 17 (1994) Cm 2559.

4. Market Access

(i)   The Agreement concentrates on replacing Non-Tariff Border Measures (NTBMs) with tariffs which provide the same level of protection. This process of replacement is known as "tariffication".

(ii)   Tariffs on agricultural products, including tariffs that have resulted from tariffication, are to be reduced by an average of 36 per cent in the case of developed countries and 24 per cent in the case of developing countries.

(iii)   The reductions described at para 4(ii) above are to be carried out over a period of six years and they are expected to begin to take effect from 1st July 1995.

(iv)   A country can maintain NTBM restrictions under the following circumstances:

    – Where no export subsidies have been applied to the imported product since the beginning of the base period of 1968-1988.

- Where inports of a given product comprise less than 3 per cent of domestic consumption again using the base period mentioned above.

- Any production restrictions that applied to a product can only be applied to the primary agricultural product and not to any products that have been prepared or worked from the primary product.

- Where the products are designated as having special treatment under non-trade concerns such as environmental or food security measures.

- A minimum market access level for a product is set at 4 per cent of domestic consumption and is increased by 0.8 per cent per year to reach 8 per cent of domestic consumption over the phase in a period of six years.

(v)   The tariffication package also provides for the maintenance of access opportunities and the establishment of minimum access tariff quotas where current access is less than 3 per cent of domestic consumption. These minimum access tariff quotas are to be expanded to 5 per cent over the implementation period.

(vi) In the case of "tariffied" products special safeguards are provided.

5. Enforcement and remedies
Once the process of tariffication has converted NTBMs into tariffs then the enforcement rules and remedies laid down by GATT 1994 are applicable as they are for other products. See Chapters 2 and 3 above and Case Study C at Chapter 10 below.

Chapter 10

Remedies – Case Studies

1. This Chapter provides three separate Case Studies covering copyright, trade in banking services and trade in clothing to illustrate the remedies available to a private sector body which is being denied its rights under GATT 1994. The usual denial of rights would occur where an importing participating Nation was failing to apply the provisions of GATT 1994 to the particular service or trade in which the private sector body was engaged.

2. It should be appreciated that GATT was conceived as a system to enable the government of the "exporting" country to obtain redress against the government of an "importing" country where the "importing" country had broken the rules of GATT. Usually, however, the body which will have suffered pecuniary loss will be a private sector body which will not have direct access to the government to government dispute settlement procedures. See Chapters 1 and 2 above. A private body therefore, must be conversant with both the public remedies and the private law remedies available to it, if it wishes to obtain redress.

3. While generally the GATT trading system is a government to government system, GATT 1994 provides for the first time both in the TRIPS agreement and to a lesser extent, in the Agreement on Trade in Services opportunities for a private sector body to bring proceedings in the domestic courts and tribunals of the "importing" country. See Chapters 4,5 and 6 above.

4. Since GATT provides in the main a framework for the "exporting" country to complain about the transgressions of the "importing" country, then even if the importing nation is found "guilty" by the WTO and the DSB the private sector body will not directly be able to recover compensation for its pecuniary loss. It will be for the government of the "exporting" country to seek to protect the interests of the private sector body by trying to ensure that the compensating redress will be of benefit

to the private sector body in its trade with the "importing" nation. See paragraph (vii) of Chapter 2 above.

5. Case Study A

Copyright

X Ltd, a company resident in the United Kingdom publishes, distributes and exports books. It discovers that its books are being published and sold in Country Y without its permission or authorisation and without the payment of royalties due to it under its copyrights. X Ltd would be advised to consider taking the following action.

(a)   Its advisers should ascertain whether Country Y is a participating Nation of GATT 1994 and has signed the WTO Agreement. This can be done by a telephone call to the Department of Trade and Industry which is the sponsoring Department within Her Majesty's Government for matters relating to GATT and the WTO. The present relevant telephone number is (0171) 215 6158.

(b)   If Country Y is a participating member of GATT and the WTO then X Ltd's advisers should seek professional advice in Country Y with regard to the possibility of bringing a direct action in the courts or tribunals of Country Y against those who are infringing X Ltd's copyrights. Reference should be made in particular to the TRIPS Agreement. See Chapter 4 above.

(c)   It may well be that Country Y has put in place adequate legal and administrative systems to enable X Ltd to bring proceedings in accordance with TRIPS so that X Ltd is able to recover damages and/or obtain other redress in Country Y in respect of the infringement of its copyrights. See in particular section 2 of TRIPS Agreement which is reproduced at Appendix II below. Proceedings brought in this way might well provide X Ltd with a speedier remedy and better compensation than would be provided by the legal/diplomatic framework of the WTO and the DSB. See Chapters 2 and 3 above.

(d)   If the necessary framework of courts or tribunals is not in place in accordance with the TRIPS Agreement in Country Y or if, notwithstanding the existence of such framework, there is no certainty that the government of Country Y is prepared to ensure that there will be no future transgressions, then X Ltd's advisers will have to consider approaching the United Kingdom government with a view to persuading it to commence proceedings under GATT against the government of Country Y.

(e)   Since both the United Kingdom and the "European Communities" have signed the Final Act at Marrakesh, see Appendix I below, consideration should also be given to the role played in these matters by the European Commission. Under the Treaty of Rome it is the European Commission which negotiates on external trading matters on behalf of the countries of the EC.

(f)   X Ltd's professional advisers accordingly are recommended not only to approach the Department of Trade and Industry but also to approach the relevant section of the Commission. The best course would be to get in touch with the Chef de Cabinet of the External Trade Commissioner. At the present time the relevant telephone number is (010) 322 296 0125.

(g)   It may well be that the DTI, on behalf of the United Kingdom government and/or the European Commission will be able to persuade the government of Country Y to put matters right and ensure that Country Y grants redress. If so, that will be the end of the matter.

(h)   If, however, Country Y is not prepared to remedy the matter through the usual diplomatic channels then X Ltd's advisers will need to persuade the DTI and the EC to invoke the dispute settlement procedures of the WTO. See Chapters 2 and 3 above.

(i)   X Ltd's advisers, however, should be aware that the decision to invoke those procedures either by the United Kingdom government and/or the European Commission is a matter within their discretion. It is an administrative/political decision. X Ltd's advisers, therefore, would be well advised to prepare thorough written submissions of the case including all the evidence of transgressions which can then be presented to the DTI and the EC in support of a request that they should invoke the dispute settlement procedure of the WTO in respect of Country Y.

(j)   It is likely that the decision whether to invoke the procedures will initially be taken by the "Article 113" Committee of the Council of Ministers. A representative of the United Kingdom government will be on this committee. It will be imperative therefore that X Ltd should have presented a cogent case to the DTI before the appropriate Minister attends the Article 113 Committee. Once a decision to invoke the procedure has been taken, then the case will be passed to the Commission which would then, possibly in conjunction with the DTI, "represent" X Ltd in the GATT panels.

(k)   Since, as explained at paragraph (i) above, the decision by the DTI and/or the EC whether to invoke the WTO procedures will be their decision over which they will have a discretion, it may be advisable, to seek support from the appropriate trade association, if any, or from the relevant member of Parliament or member of the European Parliament to assist in the task of convincing the DTI and/or the EC that they should take up the case.

(l)   If the DTI and/or the EC decide to invoke the dispute settlement procedures of the WTO then the timetable will be governed by the provisions set out in the Agreement establishing the WTO. See HMSO reference Misc No. 15(1994) Cm 2571; see also the working procedures as set out at Appendix VI below.

(m)   Again it would be advisable for X Ltd's advisers to seek to be present alongside the officials of the DTI and/or EC during all the hearings held by the Dispute Settlement Body of the WTO. It should be noted that paragraph 2 of the Working Procedures allows the panel to invite "interested parties", as well as the actual parties to the dispute. The parties to the dispute will be the two governments but advisers acting for X Ltd could certainly be described as "interested parties". If the DTI and/or EC refuse a request by advisers to be present consideration should be given to asking the WTO directly in Geneva for an invitation to the Panel meetings.

(n) The advisers of X Ltd will also be well advised to try and ensure that when the matter comes to a conclusion and if the DTI and/or the EC have succeeded in their case against Country Y, that the remedies which are pronounced are those that are most favourable to X Ltd.

(o) As stated at paragraph 7 of Chapter 2 above there are three separate verdicts that could be issued. Obviously from the point of view of X Ltd the best result would be a request from the WTO that Country Y should bring its domestic measures into conformity with the rules of the WTO Agreement. The other remedies mentioned at paragraph 7 of Chapter 2 above namely, the offer of compensatory market access to the United Kingdom government or the retaliatory withdrawal of market access by the complaining member, that is the United Kingdom government, would be of less direct benefit to X Ltd. It is, therefore, in X Ltd's interest to try and ensure again that the officials of the DTI and/or the EC press for the remedy most favourable to X Ltd.

(p) If the DTI/EC is successful, then X Ltd should, on the strength of that verdict, seek to recover damages in the courts of country Y for that country's failure to comply with its GATT obligations.

(q) As stated at paragraph (i) above the decision of the DTI and/or the EU to invoke the dispute resolution procedures of the WTO is an administrative/political decision. It may be that the bodies concerned would conclude that for other diplomatic or political reasons they would not wish to pursue such a claim against the country Y. In that case X Ltd would be without a remedy if it were unable to obtain domestic remedies in Country Y. It would then be for the consideration of X Ltd's legal advisers whether to seek by way of *Judicial Review* redress against the United Kingdom government and/or the EC for a failure to take up the case. It is outside the province of this book to consider whether Judicial Review would be applicable but the courts might be reluctant to interfere with what was seen to be an administrative/political decision unless it could be convincingly shown that the decision of the DTI and/or the EC was so unreasonable that a reasonable person could not have come to that conclusion. Despite the difficulties of obtaining Judicial Review, X Ltd's legal advisers might feel that that was the only course available to them.

6. Case Study B

Banking

A Ltd is a company resident in the United Kingdom which provides banking services worldwide. It seeks to set up a branch in country B. It is refused authorisation by the government of country B. A Ltd's advisers should consider taking the following steps.

(a) The provisions of the General Agreement on Trade in Services should be consulted. See HMSO reference, Misc. No 28 (1994) Cm 2556; Appendix III below; and the Second Annex on Financial Services and the Understanding on Commitments on Financial Services at Appendix IV below; See also Chapter 6 above.

(b) Further, there should be a close analysis of the Schedules published by the importing nation regarding Market Access, Most-Favoured Nation status and Transparency. See Chapter 6 above. These Schedules establish the limits of the restrictions which the importing nation is allowed to put upon Market Access, Transparency and Most-Favoured Nation status in respect of trade in Financial Services. These schedules are available at government libraries whose names are listed at Appendix V below.

(c) If the action of country B in refusing permission to A Ltd to set up a branch is allowed by the restrictions which are contained in the published Schedules then that is the end of the matter. If, however, the published Schedules do not contain the authorisation to restrict the setting up of branches then the advisers to A Ltd should consider the following further action.

(d) A Ltd's advisers should now consider how far the domestic courts or tribunals of country B can be used to challenge the failure to give authorisation. Article 6 of the Agreement on Trade in Services provides that each participating member of GATT should ensure that all measures of general application affecting trade in services are administered in a reasonable objective and impartial manner. A Ltd's advisers should consult professional advisers in country B to see whether advantage can be taken of Article 6 to force the authorities of country B to change their mind and grant authorisation. See Chapters 5 and 6 above and Appendix III below.

(e) If country B has failed to set up procedures to enable A Ltd to challenge the refusal of authorisation and if it can be shown that country B has failed properly to apply the provisions of Article 6, then consideration should be given to invoking the dispute settlement procedures of the WTO.

(f) The course of action to be taken by A Ltd should it decide to seek to invoke the WTO procedures is similar to the course of action which is recommended above in Case Study A at paragraphs (d)-(q) inclusive above. The steps set out in those paragraphs should then be taken.

7. Case Study C

Trade in Clothing

Z Ltd is a company which exports clothing from the United Kingdom to various countries in the world. Z Ltd believes that country C is still maintaining too high a quota in respect of the imports of clothing following country C's signing of the GATT 1994 Agreement. Z Ltd's advisers should consider taking the following steps.

(a)   The GATT 1994 established the phasing out of the Multi-Fibre Arrangement and its incorporation into a system of tariffs. These quotas are to be phased out and the tariffs to be phased in over a period of time. See Chapter 8 above for a description of the incorporation of the Multi-Fibre Agreement into GATT 1994.

(b)   Z Ltd's advisers should refer to the Agreement on Textiles and Clothing which can be obtained at HMSO on reference Misc 18 (1994) Cm 2561. If it appears from that Agreement that country C is in breach of its GATT obligations then Z Ltd's advisers should contact the DTI to make a formal complaint. Trade in textiles is dealt with at the present date by an officer of the DTI whose telephone number of (0171) 215 6373.

(c)   It should be appreciated that unlike the TRIPS Agreement and the Agreement on Trade in Services, there is no general provision in the Agreement on Textiles which would enable Z Ltd seek redress in the courts of country C. Z Ltd therefore should consider whether to ask the DTI and/or the EU to invoke the dispute settlement procedures of the WTO.

(d)   The steps which then have to be taken are similar to those mentioned and set out in Case Study A at paragraphs (d)-(q) inclusive above.

Appendix 1

Participating Nations

Algeria

Angola

Antigua & Barbuda

Argentina

Australia

Austria

Bahrain

Bangladesh

Barbados

Belgium

Belize

Benin

Bolivia

Botswana

Brazil

Brunei

Burundi

Cameroon

Canada

Central African Republic

Chile

China

Colombia

Congo

Costa Rica

Cote d'Ivoire

Cuba

Cyprus

Czech Republic

Denmark

Dominican Republic

Egypt

El Salvador

European Communities

Fiji

Finland

France

Gabon

Germany

Ghana

Greece

Guatemala

Guinea-Bissau

Guyana

Honduras

Hong Kong

Hungary

Iceland

India

Indonesia

Ireland

Israel

Italy

Jamaica

Japan

Kenya

Korea

Kuwait, Republic of

Liechtenstein

Luxembourg

Macau

Madagascar

Malawi
Malaysia
Mali
Malta
Mauritania
Mauritius
Mexico
Morocco
Mozambique
Myanmar
Namibia
Netherlands
New Zealand
Nicaragua
Niger
Nigeria
Norway
Pakistan
Paraguay
Peru
Philippines
Poland
Portugal
Qatar
Romania
Saint Lucia
Senegal
Singapore
Slovak Republic
South Africa
Spain
Sri Lanka
Suriname
Sweden
Switzerland

Tanzania
Thailand
Trinidad & Tobago
Tunisia
Turkey
UAE
Uganda
United Kingdom
USA
Uruguay
Venezuela
Zaire
Zambia
Zimbabwe

Appendix II

Extracts from TRIPS (HMSO: Misc (1994) (Cm. 2557))

PART 1
GENERAL PROVISIONS AND BASIC PRINCIPLES

Article 1
Nature and Scope of Obligations

1. Members shall give effect to the provisions of this Agreement. Members may, but shall not be obliged to implement in their law more extensive protection than is required by this Agreement, provided that such protection does not contravene the provisions of this Agreement. Members shall be free to determine the appropriate method of implementing the provisions of this Agreement within their own legal systems and practice.

2. For the purposes of this Agreement, the term "intellectual property" refers to all categories of intellectual property that are the subject of Sections 1 through 7 of Part II.

3. Members shall accord the treatment provided for in this Agreement to the nationals of other Members[1]. In respect of the relevant intellectual property right, the nationals of other Members shall be understood as those natural or legal persons that would meet the criteria for eligibility for protection provided for in the Paris Convention (1967), the Berne Convention (1971), the Rome Convention and the Treaty on Intellectual

---

[1] When "nationals" are referred to in this Agreement, they shall be deemed, in the case of a separate customs territory Member of the WTO, to mean persons, natural or legal, who are domiciled or who have a real and effective industrial or commercial establishment in that customs territory.

Property in Respect of Integrated Circuits, were all Members of the WTO members of those conventions.[2] Any Member availing itself of the possibilities provided in paragraph 3 of Article 5 or paragraph 2 of article 6 of the Rome Convention shall make a notification as foreseen in those provisions to the Council for Trade-Related Aspects of Intellectual Property Rights (the "Council for TRIPS").

Article 2
Intellectual Property Conventions

1. In respect of Parts II, III and IV of this Agreement, Members shall comply with Articles 1 through 12, and Article 19, of the Paris Convention (1967).

2. Nothing in Parts I to IV of this Agreement shall derogate from existing obligations that Members may have to each other under the Paris Convention, the Berne Convention, the Rome Convention and the Treaty on Intellectual Property in Respect of Integrated Circuits.

---

[2] In this Agreement, " Paris Convention" refers to the Paris Convention for the Protection of Industrial Property ; " Paris Convention (1967)" refers to the Stockholm Act of this Convention of 14 July 1967. "Berne Convention" refers to the Paris Act of this Convention of 24 JUly 1971. "Rome Convention" refers to the International Convention for the Protection of Performers, Producers of Phonograms and Broadcasting Organisations, adopted at Rout on 26 October 1961. "Treaty on Intellectual Property in Respect of Integrated Circuits" (IPIC Treaty) refers to the Treaty on Intellectual Property in Respect of Integrated Circuits, adopted at Washington on 26 May 1989. "WTO Agreement" refers to the Agreement Establishing the WTO.

Article 3
National Treatment

1. Each Member shall accord to the nationals of other Members treatment no less favourable than that it accords to its own nationals with regard to the protection[3] on intellectual property, subject to the exceptions already provided in, respectively, the Paris Convention (1967), the Berne Convention (1971), the Rome Convention or the Treaty on Intellectual Property in Respect on Integrated Circuits. In respect of performers, producers of phonograms and broadcasting organisations, this obligation only applies in respect of the rights provided under this Agreement. Any Member availing itself of the possibilities provided in Article 6 of the Berne Convention (1971) or paragraph 1(b) of Article 16 of the Rome Convention shall make a notification as foreseen in those provision to the Council for TRIPS.

2 Members may avail themselves of the exceptions permitted under paragraph 1 in relation to judicial and administrative procedures, including the designation of an address for service or the appointment of an agent within the jurisdiction of a Member, only where such exceptions are necessary to secure compliance with laws and regulations which are not inconsistent with the provision of this Agreement and where such practices are not applied in a manner which would constitute a disguised restriction on trade.

[3] For the purposes of Articles 3 and 4, "protection" shall include matters affecting the availability, acquisition, scope maintenance and enforcement of intellectual property rights as well as those matters affecting the use of intellectual property rights specifically addressed in this Agreement.

Article 4
Most-Favoured-Nation Treatment

With regard to the protection of intellectual property, any advantage, favour, privilege or immunity granted by a Member to the nationals of any other country shall be accorded immediately and unconditionally to the nationals of all other Members. Exempted from this obligation are any advantage, favour, privilege or immunity accorded by a Member:

(a)   deriving from international agreements on judicial assistance or law enforcement of a general nature and not particularly confined to the protection of intellectual property;

(b)   granted in accordance with the provision of the Berne Convention (1971) or the Rome Convention authorising that the treatment accorded be a function not of national treatment but of the treatment accorded in another country;

(c)   in respect of the rights of performers, producers of phonograms and broadcasting organisations not provided under this Agreement;

(d)   deriving from international agreement related to the protection of intellectual property which entered into force prior to the entry into force of the WTO Agreement, provided that such agreements are notified to the Council for TRIPS and not constitute an arbitrary or unjustifiable discrimination against nationals of other Members.

Article 5
Multilateral Agreements on Acquisition or Maintenance of Protection

The obligations under Articles 3 and 4 do not apply to procedures provided in multilateral agreements concluded under the auspices of WIPO relating to the acquisition or maintenance of intellectual property rights.

Article 6
Exhaustion

For the purposes of dispute settlement under this Agreement, subject to the provision of Articles 3 and 4 nothing in this Agreement shall be used to address the issue of the exhaustion of intellectual property rights.

PART II
STANDARDS CONCERNING THE AVAILABILITY, SCOPE AND USE OF INTELLECTUAL PROPERTY RIGHTS

SECTION 1: COPYRIGHT AND RELATED RIGHTS

Article 9
Relation to the Berne Convention

1. Members shall comply with Article 1 through 21 of the Berne Convention (1971) and the Appendix thereto. However, Members shall not have rights or obligations under this Agreement in respect of the rights conferred under Article 6bis of that Convention or of the rights derived therefrom.

2. Copyright protection shall extend to expressions and not to ideas, procedure, methods of operation or mathematical concepts as such.

Article 10
Computer Programs and Compilations of Data

1. Computer programmes, whether in source or object code, shall be protected as literary works under the Berne Convention (1971).

2. Compilations of data or other material, whether in machine readable or other form, which by reason of the selection of arrangement of their contents constitute intellectual creations shall be protected as such. Such protection, which shall not extend to the data or material itself, shall be without prejudice to any copyright subsisting in the data or material itself.

Article 11
Rental Rights

In respect of at least computer programs and cinematographic works, a Member shall provide authors and their successors in title the right to authorise or to prohibit the commercial rental to the public of originals or copies of their copyright works. A Member shall be excepted from this obligation in respect of cinematographic works unless such rental has led to widespread copying of such works which is materially impairing the exclusive right of reproduction conferred in that Member on authors and their successors in title. In respect of computer programs, this obligation does not apply to rentals where the program itself is not the essential object of the rental.

Article 12
Term of Protection

Whenever the term of protection of a work , other than a photographic work or a work of applied art, is calculated on a basis other than the life of a natural person, such term shall be no less than 50 years from the end of the calendar year of authorised publication, or, failing such authorised publication within 50 years from the making of the work, 50 years from the end of the calendar year of making.

Article 13
Limitations and Exceptions

Members shall confine limitation or exceptions to exclusive rights to certain special cases which do not conflict with a normal exploitation of the work and do not unreasonably prejudice the legitimate interest of their right holder.

Article 14
Protection of Performer, Producers of Phonograms (Sound Recording) and Broadcasting Organisation

1. In respect of a fixation of their performance on a phonogram, performers shall have the possibility of preventing the following acts when undertaken without their authorisation: the fixation of their unfixed performance and the reproduction of such fixation. Performers shall also have the possibility of preventing the following acts when undertaken without their authorisation: the broadcasting by wireless means and the communication to the public of their live performance.

2. Producers of phonograms shall enjoy the right to authorise or prohibit the direct or indirect reproduction of their phonograms.

3. Broadcasting organisations shall have the right to prohibit the following acts when undertaken without their authorisation: the fixation, the reproduction of fixations, and the rebroadcasting by wireless means of broadcasts, as well as the communication to the public of television broadcasts of the same. Where Members do not grant such rights to broadcasting organisations, they shall provide owners of copyright in the subject matter of broadcasts with the possibility of preventing the above acts, subject to the provisions of the Berne Convention (1971).

4. The provisions of Article 11 in respect of computer programs shall apply *mutatis mutandi*s to producers of phonograms and any other right holders in phonograms as determined in a Member's law. If on 15 April 1994 a Member has in force a system of equitable remuneration of right holders in respect of the rental of phonograms, it may maintain such system provided that the commercial rental of phonograms is not giving rise to the material impairment of the exclusive rights of reproduction of right holders.

5. The term of the protection available under this Agreement to performers and producers of phonograms shall last at least until the end of a period

of 50 years from the end of the calendar year in which the broadcast took place. The term of protection granted pursuant to paragraph 3 shall last for at least 20 years from the end of the calendar year in which the broadcast took place.

6. Any Member may, in relation to the rights conferred under paragraphs 1, 2 and 3, provide for conditions, limitation, exceptions and reservations to the extent permitted by the Rome Convention. However, the provision of Article 18 of the Berne Convention (1971) shall also apply, mutatis mutandis, to the rights of performers and producers of phonograms in phonograms.

SECTION 2: TRADEMARKS

Article 15
Protectable Subject Matter

1. Any sign, or any combination of signs, capable of distinguishing the goods and services of one undertaking from those of other undertakings, shall be capable of constituting a trademark. Such signs, in particular words including personal names, letters, numerals, figurative elements and combinations of colours as well as any combination of such signs, shall be eligible for registration as trademarks. Where signs are not inherently capable of distinguishing the relevant goods or services, Members may make registrability depend on distinctiveness acquired through use. Members amy require, as a condition of registration, that signs be visually perceptible.

2. Paragraph 1 shall not be understood to prevent a Member from denying registration of a trademark on other grounds, provided that they do not derogate from the provisions of the Paris Convention (1967).

3. Members may make registrability depend on use. However, actual use of a trademark shall not be a condition for filing an application for registration. An application shall not be refused solely on the ground that

intended use has not taken place before the expiry of a period of three years from the date of application.

4. The nature of the goods or services to which a trademark is to be applied shall in no case form an obstacle to registration of the trademark.

5. Members shall publish each trademark either before it is registered or promptly after it is registered and shall afford a reasonable opportunity for petitions to cancel the registration. In addition,Members may afford an opportunity for the registration of a trademark to be opposed.

Article 16
Rights Conferred

1. The owner of a registered trademark shall have the exclusive right to prevent all third parties not having the owner's consent from using in the course of trade identical or similar signs for goods or services which are identical or similar to those in respect of which the trademark is registered where such use would result in a likelihood of confusion. In case of the use of an identical sign for identical goods or services, a likelihood of confusion shall be presumed. The rights described above shall not prejudice any existing prior rights, not shall they affect the possibility of Members making rights available on the basis of use.

2. Article 6bis of the Paris Convention (1967) shall apply, *mutatis mutandis*, to services. In determining whether a trademark is well-known, Members shall take account of the knowledge of the trademark in the relevant sector of the public, including knowledge in the Member concerned which has been obtained as a result of the promotion of the trademark.

3. Article 6bis of the Paris Convention (1967) shall apply, *mutatis mutandis*, to goods or services which are not similar to those in respect of which a trademark is registered, provided that use of that trademark in relation to those goods or services would indicate a connection

between those goods or services and the owner of the registered trademark and provided that the interests of the owner of the registered trademark are likely to be damaged by such use.

Article 17
Exceptions

Members may provide limited exceptions to the rights conferred by a trademark, such as fair use of descriptive terms, provided that such exceptions take account of the legitimate interests of the owner of the trademark and of third parties.

Article 18
Term of Protection

Initial registration, and each renewal of registration, of a trademark shall be for a term of no less than seven years. The registration of a trademark shall be renewable indefinitely.

Article 19
Requirement of Use

1. If use is required to maintain a registration, the registration may be cancelled only after an uninterrupted period of at least three years of non-use, unless valid reasons based on the existence of obstacles to such use are shown by the trademark owner. Circumstances arising independently of the will of the owner of the trademark which constitute an obstacle to the use of the trademark, such as import restrictions on or other government requirements for goods or services protected by the trademark, shall be recognised as valid reasons for non-use.

2. When subject to the control of its owner, use of a trademark by another person shall be recognised as use of the trademark for the purpose of maintaining the registration.

Article 20
Other Requirements

The use of a trademark in the course of trade shall not be justifiably encumbered by special requirements, such as use with another trademark, use in a special form or use in a manner detrimental to its capability to distinguish the goods or services of one undertaking from those of other undertakings. This will not preclude a requirement prescribing the use of the trademark identifying the undertaking producing goods or services along with, but without linking it to, the trademark distinguishing the specific goods or services in question of that undertaking.

Article 21
Licensing and Assignment

Members may determine conditions on the licensing and assignment of trademarks, it being understood that the compulsory licensing of trademarks shall not be permitted and that the owner of a registered trademark shall have the right to assign the trademark with or without the transfer of the business to which the trademark belongs.

SECTION 4 : INDUSTRIAL DESIGNS

Article 25
Requirements for Protection

1. Members shall provide for the protection of independently created industrial designs that are new or original. Members may provide that designs are not new or original if they do not significantly differ from known designs or combinations of known design features. Members may provide that such protection shall not extend to designs dictated essentially by technical or functional considerations.

2. Each Member shall ensure that requirements for securing protection for textile designs, in particular in regard to any cost, examination or

publication, do not unreasonably impair the opportunity to seek and obtain such protection. Members shall be free to meet this obligation through industrial design law or through copyright law.

Article 26
Protection

1. The owner of a protected industrial design shall have the right to prevent parties not having the owner's consent from making, selling or importing articles bearing or embodying a design which is a copy, or substantially a copy, of the protected design, when such acts are undertaken for commercial purposes.

2. Members may provide limited exceptions to the protection of industrial designs, provided that such exceptions do not unreasonably conflict with the normal exploitation of protected industrial designs and do not unreasonably prejudice the legitimate interests of the owner of the protected design, taking account of the legitimate interests of third parties.

3. The duration of protection available shall amount to at least 10 years.

SECTION 5: PATENTS

Article 27
Patentable Subject Matter

1. Subject to the provision of paragraphs 2 and 3, patents shall be available for any inventions, whether products or processes, in all fields of technology, provided that they are new, involve an inventive step and are capable of industrial application.[5] Subject to paragraph 4 of Article 65, paragraph 8 of Article 70 and paragraph 3 of this Article, patents shall be available and patent rights enjoyable without discrimination as to the place of invention, the field of technology and whether products are imported or locally produced.

2. Members may exclude from patentability inventions, the prevention within their territory of the commercial exploitation of which is necessary to protect *ordre public* or morality, including to protect human, animal or plant life or health or to avoid serious prejudice to the environment, provided that such exclusion is not made merely because the exploitation is prohibited by their law.

3. Members may also exclude from patentability:
   (a) diagnostic, therapeutic and surgical methods for the treatment of humans or animals;
   (b) plants and animals other than micro-organisms, and essentially biological processes for the production of plants or animals other then non-biological and microbiological processes. However, Members shall provide for the protection of plant varieties either by patents or by an effective *sui generis* or by any combination thereof. The provision of this subparagraph shall be reviewed four years after the date of entry into force of the WTO Agreement.

[5] For the purposes of this Article, the terms "inventive step" and "capable of industrial application" may be deemed by a Member to be synonymous with the terms "non-obvious" and "useful" respectively.

Article 28
Rights Conferred

1. A patent shall confer on its owner the following exclusive rights:
   (a) where the subject matter of a patent is a product, to prevent third parties not having the owner's consent from the acts of: making, using, offering for sale, selling, or importing[6] for these purposes that product;
   (b) where the subject matter of a patent is a process, to prevent third parties not having the owner's consent from the act of using the process, and from the acts of: using, offering for sale, selling, or importing for these purposes at least the product obtained directly by that process.

2. Patent owners shall also have the right to assign, or transfer by succession, the patent and to conclude licensing contracts.

Article 29
Conditions on Patent Applicants

1. Members shall require that an applicant for a patent shall disclose the invention in a manner sufficiently clear and complete for the invention to be carried out by a person skilled in the art and may require the applicant to indicate the best mode for carrying out the invention known to the inventor at the filing date or, where priority is claimed, at the priority date of the application.

2. Members may require an applicant for a patent to provide information concerning the applicant's corresponding foreign applications and grants.

---

[6] This right, like all other rights conferred under this Agreement in respect of the use, sale, importation of other distribution of goods, is subject to the provisions of Article 6.

Article 30
Exceptions to Rights Conferred

Members may provide limited exceptions to the exclusive rights conferred by a patent, provided that such exceptions do not unreasonably conflict with a normal exploitation of the patent and do not unreasonably prejudice the legitimate interests of the patent owner, taking account of the legitimate interests of third parties.

Article 31
Other Use Without Authorisation of the Right Holder

Where the law of a Member allows for other use[7] of the subject matter of a patent without the authorisation of the right holder, including use by the government or third parties authorised by the government, the following provision shall be respected:

(a) authorisation of such use shall be considered on its individual merits;

(b) such use may only be permitted if, prior to such use, the proposed user has made efforts to obtain authorisation from the right holder on reasonable commercial terms and conditions and that such efforts have not been successful within a reasonable period of time. This requirement may be waived by a Member in the case of a national emergency or other circumstances of extreme urgency, the right holder shall, nevertheless, be notified as soon as reasonably practicable. In the case of public non-commercial use, where the government or contractor, without making a patent search, knows or has demonstrable ground to know that a valid patent is or will be used by or for the government, the right holder shall be informed promptly;

[7] "Other use" refers to use other than that allowed under Article 30.

(c) the scope and duration of such use shall be limited to the purpose for which it was authorised, and in the case of semi-conductor technology shall only be for public non-commercial use or to remedy a practice determined after judicial or administrative process to be anti-competitive;

(d) such use shall be no-exclusive;

(e) such use shall be non-assignable, except with that part of the enterprise or goodwill which enjoys such use;

(f) any such use shall be authorised predominantly for the supply of the domestic market of the Member authorising such use;

(g) authorisation for such use shall be liable, subject to adequate protection of the legitimate interests of the persons so authorised, to be terminated if and when the circumstances which led to it cease to exist and are unlikely to recur. The competent authority shall have the authority to review, upon motivated request, the continued existence of these circumstances;

(h) the right holder shall be paid adequate remuneration in the circumstances of each case, taking into account the economic value of the authorisation;

(i) the legal validity of any decision relating to the authorisation of such use shall be subject to judicial review or other independent review by and distinct higher authority in that Member;

(j) any decision relating to the remuneration provided in respect of such use shall be subject to judicial review or other independent review by a distinct higher authority in that Member;

(k) Members are not obliged to apply the conditions set forth in subparagraphs (b) and (f) where such use is permitted to remedy a practice determined after judicial or administrative process to be anti-competitive. The need to correct anti-competitive practices may be taken into account in determining the amount of remuneration in such cases. Competent authorities shall have the authority to refuse termination of authorisation if and when the conditions which led to such authorisation are likely to recur;

(l) where such use is authorised to permit the exploitation of a patent ("the second patent") which cannot be exploited without infringing another patent ("the first patent"), the following additional conditions shall apply:

   (i)   the invention claimed in the second patent shall involve an important technical advance of considerable economic significance in relation to the invention claimed in the first patent;

   (ii)   the owner of the first patent shall be entitle to a cross-license on reasonable terms to use the invention claimed in the second patent; and

   (iii) the use authorised in respect of the first patent shall be non-assignable except with the assignment of the second patent.

Article 32
Revocation/Forfeiture
An opportunity for judicial review of any decision to revoke or forfeit a patent shall be available.

Article 33
Term of Protection
The term of protection available shall not end before the expiration of a period of twenty years counted from the filing date.[8]

---

[8] It is understood that those Members which do not have a system of original grant may provide that the term of protection shall be computed from the filing date in the system of original grant.

Article 34
Process Patents: Burden of Proof

1. For the purposes of civil proceedings in respect of the infringement of the rights of the owner referred to in paragraph 1(b) of Article 28, if the subject matter of a patent is a process for obtaining a product, the judicial authorities shall have the authority to order the defendant to prove that the process to obtain an identical product is different from the patented process. Therefore, Members shall provide, in at least one of the following circumstances, that any identical product when produced without the consent of the patent owner shall, in the absence of proof to the contrary, be deemed to have been obtained by the patented process:

   (a) if the product obtained by the patented process is new;
   (b) if there is a substantial likelihood that the identical product was made by the process and the owner of the patent has been unable through reasonable efforts to determine the process actually used.

2. Any Member shall be free to provide that the burden of proof indicated in paragraph 1 shall be on the alleged infringer only if the condition referred to in subparagraph (a) is fulfilled or only if the condition referred to in subparagraph (b) is fulfilled

3. In the adduction of proof to the contrary, the legitimate interests of defendants in protecting their manufacturing and business secrets shall be taken into account.

SECTION 6: LAYOUT-DESIGN (TOPOGRAPHIES) OF INTEGRATED CIRCUITS

Article 35
Relation to the IPIC Treaty

Members agree to provide protection to the layout-designs (topographies) of integrated circuits (referred to in this Agreement as "layout-designs") in accordance with Articles 2 through 7 (other than paragraph 3 of Article 6), Article 12 and paragraph 3 of Article 16 of the Treaty on Intellectual Property in Respect of Integrated Circuits and, in addition, to comply with the following provisions.

Article 36
Scope of the Protection

Subject to the provisions of paragraph 1 of Article 37, Members shall consider unlawful the following acts if performed without the authorisation of the right holder[9]: importing, selling, or otherwise distributing for commercial purposes a protected layout-design, an integrated circuit in which a protected layout-design is incorporated, or an article incorporating such as integrated circuit only in so far as it continues to contain an unlawfully reproduced layout-design.

Article 37
Acts Not Requiring the Authorisation of the Right Holder

1. Notwithstanding Article 36, no Member shall consider unlawful the performance of any of the acts referred to in that Article in respect of an integrated circuit incorporating an unlawfully reproduced layout-design or any article incorporating such an integrated circuit where the person performing or ordering such acts did not know and has no reasonable ground to know, when acquiring the integrated circuit or article incorporating such an integrated circuit, that it incorporated an unlawfully reproduced layout-design. Members shall provide that, after the time that such person has received sufficient notice that the layout-design was unlawfully reproduced, that person may perform any of the acts with respect to the stock on hand or ordered before such time, but shall be liable to pay to the right holder a sum equivalent to a reasonable royalty such as would be payable under a freely negotiated license in respect of such a layout-design.

[9] The term "right holder" in this Section shall be understood as having the same meaning as the term "holder of the right" in the IPIC Treaty.

2. The condition set out in subparagraphs (a) through (k) of Article 31 shall apply *mutatis mutandis* in the event of any non-voluntary licensing of a layout-design or of its use by or for the government without the authorisation of the right holder.

Article 38
Term of Protection

1. In Members requiring registration as a condition for protection, the term of protection of layout-design shall not end before the expiration of a period of 10 years counted from the date of filing an application for registration or from the first commercial exploitation wherever in the world it occurs.

2. In Members not requiring registration as a condition for protection, layout-designs shall be protected for a term of no less than 10 years from the date of the first commercial exploitation wherever in the world it occurs.

3. Notwithstanding paragraphs 1 and 2, a Member may provide that protection shall lapse 15 years after the creation of the layout-design.

PART III

ENFORCEMENT OF INTELLECTUAL PROPERTY RIGHTS

SECTION 1: GENERAL OBLIGATIONS

Article 41

1. Members shall ensure that enforcement procedures as specified in this Part are available under their law so as to permit effective action against any act of infringement of intellectual property rights covered by this Agreement, including expeditious remedies to prevent infringements and remedies which constitute a deterrent to further infringements. These

procedures shall be applied in such a manner as to avoid the creation of barriers to legitimate trade and to provide for safeguards against their abuse.

2. Procedures concerning the enforcement of intellectual property rights shall be fair and equitable. They shall not be unnecessarily complicated or costly, or entail unreasonable time-limits or unwarranted delays.

3. Decisions on the merits of a case shall preferably be in writing and reasoned. They shall be made available at least to the parties to the proceeding without undue delay. Decisions on the merits of a case shall be based only on evidence in respect of which parties were offered the opportunity to be heard.

4. Parties to a proceeding shall have an opportunity for review by a judicial authority of final administrative decision and subject to jurisdictional provisions in a Member's law concerning the importance of a case, of at least the legal aspects of initial judicial decisions on the merits of a case. However, there shall be no obligation to provide an opportunity for a review of acquittals in criminal cases.

5. It is understood that this Part does not create any obligation to put in place a judicial system for the enforcement of intellectual property rights distinct from that for the enforcement of law in general, nor does it affect the capacity of Members to enforce their law in general. Nothing in this Part creates any obligation with respect to the distribution of resources as between enforcement of intellectual property rights and the enforcement of law in general.

SECTION 2: CIVIL AND ADMINISTRATIVE PROCEDURES AND REMEDIES

Article 42
Fair and Equitable Procedures

Members shall make available to right holders[11] civil judicial procedures concerning the enforcement of any intellectual property right covered by this Agreement. Defendants shall have the right to written notice which is timely and contains sufficient detail, including the basis of the claims. Parties shall be allowed to be represented by independent legal counsel, and procedures shall not impose overly burdensome requirements concerning mandatory personal appearances. All parties to such procedures shall be duly entitled to substantiate their claims and to present all relevant evidence. The procedure shall provide a means to identify and protect confidential information, unless this would be contrary to existing constitutional requirements.

Article 43
Evidence

1. The judicial authorities shall have the authority, where a party has presented reasonably available evidence sufficient to support its claims and has specified evidence relevant to substantiation of its claims which lies in the control of the opposing party, to order that this evidence be produced by the opposing party, subject in appropriate cases to conditions which ensure the protection of confidential information.

[11] For the purpose of this Part, the term "right holder" includes federations and associations having legal standing to assert such rights.

2. In cases in which a party to a proceeding voluntarily and without good reason refuses access to, or otherwise does not provide necessary information within a reasonable period, or significantly impedes a procedure relating to an enforcement action, a Member may accord judicial authorities the authority to make preliminary and final determinations, affirmative or negative, on the basis of the information presented to them, including the complaint or the allegation presented by the party adversely affected by the denial of access to information, subject to providing the parties an opportunity to be heard on the allegation or evidence.

Article 44
Injunctions

1. The judicial authorities shall have the authority to order a party to desist from an infringement, *inter alia* to prevent the entry into the channels of commerce in their jurisdiction of imported goods that involve the infringement of an intellectual property right, immediately after customs clearance of such goods. Members are not obliged to accord such authority in respect of protected subject matter acquired or ordered by a person prior to knowing or having reasonable grounds to know that dealing in such subject matter would entail the infringement of an intellectual property right.

2. Notwithstanding the other provision of this Part and provided that provision of Part II specifically addressing use by governments, or by third parties authorised by a government, without the authorisation of the right holder are complied with,Members may limit the remedies available against such use to payment of remuneration in accordance with subparagraph (h) of Article 31. In cases, the remedies under this Part shall apply or, where these remedies are inconsistent with a Member's law, declaratory judgements and adequate compensation shall be available.

Article 45
Damages

1. The judicial authorities shall have the authority to order the infringer to pay the right holder damages adequate to compensate for the injury the right holder has suffered because of an infringement of that person's intellectual property right by an infringer who knowingly, or with reasonable grounds to know, engaged in infringing activity.

2. The judicial authorities shall also have the authority to order the infringer to pay the right holder expenses, which may include appropriate attorney's fees. In appropriate cases, Members may authorise the judicial authorities to order recovery of profits and/or payment of pre-established damages even where the infringer did not knowingly, or with reasonable grounds to know, engage in infringing activity.

Article 46
Other Remedies

In order to create an effective deterrent to infringement, the judicial authorities shall have the authority to order that goods that they have found to be infringing be, without compensation of any sort, disposed of outside the channels of commerce in such a manner as to avoid any harm caused to the right holder, or, unless this would be contrary to existing constitutional requirements, destroyed. The judicial authorities shall also have the authority to order that materials and implements the predominant use of which has been in the creation of the infringing goods be, without compensation of any sort, disposed of outside the channels of commerce in such a manner as to minimise the risks of further infringements. In considering such requests, the need for proportionality between the seriousness of the infringement and the remedies ordered as well as the interest of their parties shall be taken in to account. In regard to counterfeit trademark goods, the simple removal of the trademark unlawfully affixed shall not be sufficient, other than in exceptional cases, to permit release of the goods into the channels of commerce.

Article 47
Right of Information

Members may provide that the judicial authorities shall have the authority, unless this would be out of proportion to the seriousness of the infringement, to order the infringer to inform the right holder of the identity of third persons involved in the production and distribution of the infringing goods or services and of their channels of distribution.

Article 48
Indemnification of the Defendant

1. The judicial authorities shall have the authority to order a party at whose request measures were taken and who has abused enforcement procedures to provide a party wrongfully enjoined or restrained adequate compensation for the injury suffered because of such abuse. The judicial authorities shall also have the authority to order the applicant to pay the defendant expenses, which may include appropriate attorney's fees.

2. In respect of the administration of any law pertaining to the protection or enforcement of intellectual property rights, Members shall only exempt both public authorities and officials from liability to appropriate remedial measures where actions are taken or intended in good faith in the course of the administration of that law.

Article 49
Administrative Procedures

To the extent that any civil remedy can be ordered as a result of administrative procedures on the merits of a case, such procedures shall conform to principles equivalent in substance to those set forth in this Section.

SECTION 3 PROVISIONAL MEASURES

Article 50

1. The judicial authorities shall have the authority to order prompt and effective provisional measures:

   (a) to prevent an infringement of any intellectual property right from occurring, and in particular to prevent the entry into the channels of commerce in their jurisdiction of goods, including imported goods immediately after customs clearance;
   (b) to preserve relevant evidence in regard to the alleged infringement.

2. The judicial authorities shall have the authority to adopt provisional measure *inaudita altera parte* where appropriate, in particular where any delay is likely to cause irreparable harm to the right holder, or where there is a demonstrable risk of evidence being destroyed.

3. The judicial authorities shall have the authority to require the applicant to provide any reasonable available evidence in order to satisfy themselves with a sufficient degree of certainty that the applicant is the right holder and that the applicant's right is being infringed or that such infringement is imminent, and to order the applicant to provide a security or equivalent assurance sufficient to protect the defendant and to prevent abuse.

4. Where provisional measures have been adopted *inaudita altera parte*, the parties affected shall be given notice, without delay after the execution of the measures at the latest. A review, including a right to be heard, shall take place upon request of the defendant with a view to deciding, within a reasonable period after the notification of the measure, whether these measure shall be modified, revoked or confirmed.

5. The applicant may be required to supply other information necessary for the identification of the goods concerned by the authority that will execute the provisional measures.

6. Without prejudice to paragraph 4, provisional measures taken on the bases of paragraphs 1 and 2 shall, upon request by the defendant, be revoked or otherwise cease to have effect, if proceedings leading to a decision on the merits of the case are not initiated within a reasonable period, to be determined by the judicial authority ordering the measures where a Member's law so permits or, in the absence of such a determination, not to exceed 20 working days or 31 calendar days, whichever is the longer.

7. Where the provisional measures are revoked or where they lapse due to any act or omission by the applicant, or where it is subsequently found that there has been no infringement or threat of infringement of an intellectual property right, the judicial authorities shall have the authority to order the applicant, upon request of the defendant, to provide the defendant appropriate compensation for any injury caused by these measures.

8. To the extent that any provisional measure can be ordered as a result of administrative procedures, such procedures shall conform to principles equivalent in substance to those set forth in this Section.

SECTION 4: SPECIAL REQUIREMENTS RELATED TO BORDER MEASURES[12]

Article 51
Suspension of Release by Customs Authorities

Members shall, in conformity with the provisions set out below, adopt procedures[13] to enable a right holder, who has valid grounds for suspecting that the importation of counterfeit trademark or pirated copyright goods[14] may take place, to lodge an application in writing with competent authorities, administrative or judicial, for the suspension by the customs authorities of the release into free circulation of such goods. Members may enable such an application to be made in respect of goods which involve other infringements of intellectual property rights, provided that the requirements of this Section are met. Members may also provide for corresponding procedures concerning the suspension by the customs authorities of the release of infringing goods destined for exportation from their territories.

[12] Where a Member has dismantled substantially all controls over movement of goods across its border with another Member with which it forms part of a customs union, it shall not be required to apply the provisions of this Section at that border.

[13] It is understood that there shall be no obligation to apply such procedure to imports of goods put on the market in another country by or with the consent of the right holder, or to goods in transit.

[14] For the purposes of this Agreement:
(a) "counterfeit trademark goods" shall mean any goods, including packaging, bearing without authorisation a trademark which is identical to the trademark validly registered in respect of such goods, or which cannot be distinguished in its essential aspects from such a trademark, and which thereby infringed the rights of the owner of the trademark in question under the law of the country of importation:
(b) "pirated copyright goods" shall mean any goods which are copies made without the consent of the right holder or person duly authorised by the right holder in the country of production and which are made directly or indirectly from an article where the making of that copy would have constituted an infringement of a copyright or a related right under the law of the country of importation.

Article 52
Application

Any right holder initiating the procedures under Article 51 shall be required to provide adequate evidence to satisfy the competent authorities that, under the laws of the country of importation, there is prima facie an infringement of the right holder's intellectual property right and to supply a sufficiently detailed description of the goods to make them readily recognisable by the customs authorities. The competent authorities shall inform the applicant within a reasonable period whether they have accepted the application and, where determined by the competent authorities, the period for which the customs authorities will take action.

Article 53
Security or Equivalent Assurance

1. The competent Authorities shall have the authority to require an applicant to provide a security or equivalent assurance sufficient to protect the defendant and the competent authorities and to prevent abuse. Such security or equivalent assurance shall not unreasonably deter recourse to these procedures.

2. Where pursuant to an application under this Section the release of goods involving industrial designs, patents, layout-designs or undisclosed information into free circulation has been suspended by customs authorities on the basis of a decision other than by a judicial or other independent authority, and the period provided for in Article 55 has expired without the granting of provision relief by the duly empowered authority, and provided that all other conditions for importation have been compiled with, the owner, imported, or consignee of such goods shall be entitled to their release on the posting of a security in an amount sufficient to protect the right holder for any infringement. Payment of such security shall not prejudice any other remedy available to the right holder, it being understood that the security shall be released if the right holder fails to pursue the right of action within a reasonable period of time.

Article 54
Notice of Suspension

The importer and the applicant shall be promptly notified of the suspension of the release of goods according to Article 51.

Article 55
Duration of Suspension

If, within a period not exceeding 10 working days after the applicant has been served notice of the suspension, the customs authorities have not been informed that proceedings leading to a decision on the merits of the case have been initiated by a party other than the defendant, or that the duly empowered authority has taken provisional measures prolonging the suspension of the release of the goods, the goods shall be released, provided that all other conditions for importation or exportation have been compiled with; in appropriate cases, this time-limit may be extended by another 10 working days. If proceedings leading to a decision on the merits of the case have been initiated, a review, including a right to be heard, shall take place upon request of the defendant with a view to deciding, within a reasonable period, whether these measure shall be modified, revoked or confirmed. Notwithstanding the above, where the suspension of the release of goods is carried out or continued in accordance with a provisional judicial measure, the provision of paragraph 6 of Article 50 shall apply.

Article 56
Indemnification of the Importer and of the Owner of the Goods

Relevant authorities shall have the authority to order the applicant to pay the importer, the consignee and the owner of the goods appropriate compensation for any injury caused to them through the wrongful detention of goods or through the detention of goods released pursuant to Article 55.

Article 57
Right of Inspection and Information

Without prejudice to the protection of confidential information, Members shall provide the competent authorities the authority to give the right holder sufficient opportunity to have any goods detained by the customs authorities inspected in order to substantiate the right holder's claims. The competent authorities shall also have authority to give the importer an equivalent opportunity to have any such goods inspected. Where a positive determination has been made on the merits of a case, Members may provide the competent authorities the authority to inform the right holder of the names and addresses of the consignor, the importer and the consignee and of the quantity of the goods in questions.

Article 58
Ex Officio Action

Where Members require competent authorities to act upon their own initiative and to suspend the release of goods in respect of which they have acquired prima facie evidence that an intellectual property right is being infringed:

(a) the competent authorities may at any time seek from the right holder any information that may assist them to exercise these powers;

(b) the importer and the right holder shall be promptly notified of the suspension. Where the importer has lodged an appeal against the suspension with the competent authorities, the suspension shall be subject to the conditions, *mutatis mutandis*, set out at Article 55;

(c) Members shall only exempt both public authorities and officials from liability to appropriate remedial measures where actions are taken or intended in good faith.

Article 59
Remedies

Without prejudice to other rights of action open to the right holder and subject to the right of the defendant to seek review by a judicial authority, competent authorities shall have the authority to order the destruction or disposal of infringing goods in accordance with the principles set out in Article 46. In regard to counterfeit trademark goods, the authorities shall not allow the re-exportation of the infringing goods in an unaltered state or subject them to a different customs procedure, other than in exceptional circumstances.

Article 60
De Minimis Imports

Members may exclude from the application of the above provisions small quantities of goods of a non-commercial nature contained in travellers' personal luggage or sent in small consignments.

SECTION 5: CRIMINAL PROCEDURES

Article 61

Members shall provide for criminal procedures and penalties to be applied at least in cases of wilful trademark counterfeiting or copyright piracy on a commercial scale. Remedies available shall include imprisonment and/or monetary fines sufficient to provide a deterrent, consistently with the level of penalties applied for crimes of a corresponding gravity. In appropriate cases, remedies available shall also include the seizure, forfeiture and destruction of the infringing goods and of any materials and implements the predominant use of which has been in the commission of the offence. Members may provide for criminal procedures and penalties to be applied in other cases of infringement of intellectual property rights, in particular where they are committed wilfully and on a commercial scale.

Members was waive the obligation to notify such laws and regulations directly to the Council if consultations with WIPO on the establishment of a common register containing these laws and regulations are successful. The Council shall also consider in this connection any action required regarding notification pursuant to the obligations under this Agreement stemming from the provision of Article 6*ter* of the Paris Convention (1967)

3. Each Member shall be prepared to supply, in response to a written request from another Member, information of the sort referred to in paragraph 1. A Member, having reason to believe that a specific judicial decision or administrative ruling or bilateral agreement in the area of intellectual property rights affects its rights under this Agreement, may also request in writing to be given access to or be informed in sufficient detail of such specific judicial decisions or administrative rulings or bilateral agreements.

4. Nothing in paragraphs 1, 2 and 3 shall require Members to disclose confidential information which would impede law enforcement or otherwise be contrary to public interest or would prejudice the legitimate commercial interests of particular enterprises, public or private.

PART VI
TRANSITIONAL ARRANGEMENTS

Article 65
Transitional Arrangements

1. Subject to the provision of paragraphs 2,3, and 4, no Member shall be obliged to apply the provision of this Agreement before the expiry of a general period of one year following the date of entry into force of the WTO Agreement.

2. A developing country Member is entitled to delay for a further period of four years the date of application, as defined in paragraph 1, of the provisions of this Agreement other than Articles 3, 4 and 5.

3. Any other Member which is in the process of transformation from a centrally-planned into a market, free-enterprise economy and which is undertaking structural reform of its intellectual property system and facing special problems in the preparation and implementation of intellectual property laws and regulations, may also benefit from a period of delay as foreseen in paragraph 2.

4. To the extent that a developing country Member is obliged by this Agreement to extend product patent protection to areas of technology not so protectable in its territory on the general date of application of this Agreement for that Member, as defined in paragraph 2, it may delay the application of the provisions on product patents of Section 5 of Part II to such areas of technology for an additional period of five years.

5. A Member availing itself of a transitional period under paragraphs 1,2 3 or 4 shall ensure that any changes in its laws, regulations and practice made during that period do not result in a lesser degree of consistency with the provisions of this Agreement.

Article 66
Least-Developed Country Members

1. In view of the special needs and requirements of least-developed country Members, their economic, financial and administrative constraints, and their need for flexibility to create a viable technological base, such Members shall not be required to apply the provisions of this Agreement, other than Articles 3, 4 and 5, for a period of 10 years from the date of application as defined under paragraph 1 of Article 65. The Council for TRIPS shall, upon duly motivated request by a least-developed country Member, accord extensions of this period.

2. Developed country Members shall provide incentives to enterprises and institutions in their territories for the purpose of promoting and encouraging technology transfer to least-developed country Members in order to enable them to create a sound and viable technological base.

Article 70
Protection of Existing Subject Matter

1. This Agreement does not give rise to obligations in respect of acts which occurred before the date of application of the Agreement for the Member in question.

2. Except as otherwise provided for in this Agreement, this Agreement gives rise to obligations in respect of all subject matter existing at the date of application of this Agreement for the Members in question, and which is protected in that Member on the said date, or which meets or comes subsequently to meet the criteria for protection under the terms of this Agreement. In respect of this paragraph and paragraphs 3 and 4, copyright obligations with respect to existing works shall be solely determined under Article 18 of the Berne Convention (1971), and obligations with respect to the rights of producers of phonograms and performers in existing phonograms shall be determined solely under Article 18 of the Berne Convention (1971) as made applicable under paragraph 6 of Article 14 of this Agreement.

3. There shall be no obligation to restore protection to subject matter which on the date of application of this Agreement for the Member in question has fallen into the public domain.

4. In respect of any acts in respect of specific objects embodying protected subject matter which become infringing under the terms of legislation in conformity with this Agreement, and which were commenced, or in respect of which a significant investment was made, before the date of acceptance of the WTO Agreement by that Member, any Member may provide for a limitation of the remedies available to the right holder as to the continued performance of such acts after the date of application of this Agreement for that Member. In such cases the Member shall, however, at least provide for the payment of equitable remuneration.

5. A Member is not obliged to apply the provision of Article 11 and of paragraph 4 of Article 14 with respect to originals or copies purchased prior to the date of application of this Agreement for that Member.

6. Members shall not be required to apply Article 31, or the requirement in paragraph 1 of Article 27 that patent rights shall be enjoyable without discrimination as to the field of technology, to use without the authorisation of the right holder where authorisation for such use was granted by the government before the date this Agreement became known.

7. In the case of intellectual property rights for which protection is conditional upon registration, applications for protection which are pending on the date of application of this Agreement for the Member in question shall be permitted to be amended to claim any enhanced protection provided under the provisions of this Agreement. Such amendments shall not include new matter.

8. Where a Member does not make available as of the date of entry into force of the WTO Agreement patent protection for pharmaceutical and agricultural chemical products commensurate with its obligations under Article 27, that Member shall:

   (a) not withstanding the provisions of Part VI, provide as from the date of entry into force of the WTO Agreement a means by which applications for patents for such inventions can be filed;

   (b) apply to these applications, as of the date of application of this Agreement, the criteria for patentability as laid down in this Agreement as if those criteria were being applied on the date of filing in that Member or, where priority is available and claimed, the priority date of the application; and

   (c) provide patent protection in accordance with this Agreement as from the grant of the patent and for the remainder of the patent term, counted from the filing date in accordance with Article 33 of this Agreement, for those of these application that meet the criteria for protection referred to in subparagraph (b).

9. Where a product is the subject of a patent application in a Member in accordance with paragraph 8(a), exclusive marketing rights shall be granted, notwithstanding the provisions of Part VI, for a period of five years after obtaining marketing approval in that Member or until a product patent is granted or rejected in that Member, whichever period is shorter, provided that, subsequent to the entry into force of the WTO Agreement, a patent application has been filed and a patent granted for that product in another Member and marketing approval in such other Member.

Appendix III

External Services Agreement (HMSO MISC No. 28 (Cnd. 2556))

PART 1
SCOPE AND DEFINITION

Article I
Scope and Definition

1. This Agreement applies to measures by Members affecting trade in services.

2. For the purposes of this Agreement, trade in services is defined as the supply of a service:
   (a) from the territory of one Member into the territory of any other Member;
   (b) in the territory of one Member to the service consumer of any other Member;
   (c) by a service supplier of one Member, through commercial presence in the territory of any other Member;
   (d) by a service supplier of one Member, through presence of natural persons of a Member in the territory of any other Member.

3. For the purposes of this Agreement:
   (a) "measures by Members" means measures taken by:
   (i) central, regional or local governments and authorities; and
   (ii) non-governmental bodies in the exercise of powers delegated by central, regional or local governments or authorities;

In fulfilling its obligations and commitments under the Agreement, each Member shall take such reasonable measures as may be available to it to ensure their observance by regional local governments and authorities and non-governmental bodies within its territory;

(b) "services" includes any service in any sector except services supplied in the exercise of governmental authority;

(c) "a service supplied in the exercise of governmental authority" means any service which is supplied neither on a commercial basis, nor in competition with one or more service suppliers.

PART II
GENERAL OBLIGATIONS AND DISCIPLINES

Article II
Most-Favoured-Nation Treatment

1. With respect to any measure covered by this Agreement, each Member shall accord immediately and unconditionally to services and service suppliers of any other Member treatment no less favourable than that it accords to like services and service suppliers of any other country.

2. A Member may maintain a measure inconsistent with paragraph 1 provided that such a measure is listed in, and meets the conditions of, the Annex on Article II Exemptions.

3. The provisions of this Agreement shall not be so construed as to prevent any member from conferring or according advantages to adjacent countries in order to facilitate exchanges limited to continuous frontier zones of services that are both locally produced and consumed.

Article III
Transparency

1. Each Member shall publish promptly and, except in emergency situations, at the latest by the time of their entry into force, all relevant measures of general application which pertain to or affect the operation of this Agreement. International agreements pertaining to or affecting trade in services to which a Member is a signatory shall also be published.

2. Where publication as referred to in paragraph 1 is not practicable, such information shall be made otherwise publicly available.

3. Each Member shall promptly and at least annually inform the Council for Trade in Services of the introduction of any new, or any changes to existing, laws, regulations or administrative guidelines which significantly affected trade in services covered by its specific commitments under this Agreement.

4. Each Member shall respond promptly to all requests by any other member for specific information on any of its measures of general application or international agreements within the meaning of paragraph 1. Each Member shall also establish one or more enquiry points to provide specific information to other members, upon request, on all such matters as well as those subject to the notification requirement in paragraph 3. Such enquiry points shall be established within two years from the date of entry into force of the Agreement Establishing the WTO (referred to in this Agreement as the "WTO Agreement"). Appropriate flexibility with respect to the time-limit within which such enquiry points are to be established may be agreed upon for individual developing country Members. Enquiry points need not be depositories of laws and regulations.

5. Any Member may notify to the Council for Trade in Services any measure, taken by any other member, which it considers affects the operation of this Agreement.

ARTICLE VI
Domestic Regulation
1. In sectors where specific commitments are undertaken, each Member shall ensure that all measures of general application affecting trade in services are administered in a reasonable, objective and impartial manner.

2. (a) Each Member shall maintain or institute as soon as practicable judicial, arbitral or administrative tribunals or procedures which provide, at the request of an affected service supplier, trade in services. Where such procedures are not independent of the agency entrusted with the administrative decision concerned, the Member shall ensure that the procedures in fact provide for an objective and impartial review.

(b) The provisions of subparagraph (a) shall not be construed to require a Member to institute such tribunals or procedures where this would be inconsistent with its constitutional structure or the nature of its legal system.

3. Where authorisation is required for the supply of a service on which a specific commitment has been made, the competent authorities of a Member shall, within a reasonable period of time after the submission of an application considered complete under domestic laws and regulations, inform the applicant of the decision concerning the application. At the request of the applicant, the competent authorities of the member shall provide, without undue delay, information concerning the status of the application.

4. With a view to ensuring that measures relating to qualification requirements and procedures, technical standards and licensing requirements do not constitute unnecessary barriers to trade in Services, the Council for Trade in Services shall, through appropriate bodies it may establish, develop any necessary disciplines. Such disciplines shall aim to ensure that such requirements are, *inter alia*:

(a) based on objective and transparent criteria, such as competence and the ability to supply the service;
(b) not more burdensome than necessary to ensure the quality of the service;
(c) in the case of licensing procedures, not in themselves a restriction on the supply of the service.

5. (a) In sectors in which a Member has undertaken specific commitments, pending the entry into force of disciplines developed in these sectors pursuant to paragraph 4, the Member shall not apply licensing and qualification requirements and technical standards that nullify or impair such specific commitments in a manner which:

   (i) does not comply with the criteria outlined in subparagraphs 4(a), (b) or (c); and

   (ii) could not reasonably have been expected of that member at the time the specific commitments in those sectors were made.

   (b) in determining whether a Member is in conformity with the obligation under paragraph 5(a), account shall be taken of international standards of relevant international organisations[3] applied by that Member.

6. In sectors where specific commitments regarding professional services are undertaken, each Member shall provide for adequate procedures to verify the competence of professionals of any other Member.

Article VII
Recognition

1. For the purposes of the fulfilment, in whole or in part, of its standards or criteria for the authorisation, licensing or certification of services suppliers, and subject to the requirements of paragraph 3, a Member may recognise the education or experience obtained, requirements met,or licenses or certification granted in a particular country. Such recognition, which may be achieved through harmonisation or otherwise, may be based upon an agreement or arrangement with the country concerned or may be accorded autonomously.

---

[3] The term "relevant international organisations" refers to international bodies whose membership is open to the relevant bodies of at least all Members of the WTO.

2. A member that is a party to an agreement or arrangement of the type referred to in paragraph 1, whether existing or future, shall afford adequate opportunity for other interested Members to negotiate their accession to such an agreement or arrangement or to negotiate comparable ones with it. Where a Member accords recognition autonomously, it shall afford adequate opportunity for any other Member to demonstrate that education, experience, licenses, or certifications obtained or requirements met in that other Member's territory should be recognised.

3. A Member shall not accord recognition in a manner which would constitute a means of discrimination between countries in the application of its standards or criteria for the authorisation, licensing or certification of services suppliers, or a disguised restriction on trade in services.

4. Each Member shall:
   (a) within 12 months from the date on which the WTO Agreement takes effect for it, inform the Council for Trade in Services of its existing recognition measures and state whether such measures are based on agreements or arrangements of the types referred to in paragraph 1;
   (b) promptly inform the Council for Trade in Services as far in advance as possible of the opening of negotiations on an agreement or arrangement of the type referred to in paragraph 1 in order to provide adequate opportunity to any other Member to indicate their interest in participating in the negotiations before they enter a substantive phase;
   (c) promptly inform the Council for Trade in Services when it adopts new recognition measures or significantly modifies existing ones and state whether the measures are based on an agreement or arrangement of the type referred to in paragraph 1.

5. Wherever appropriate, recognition should be based on multilaterally agreed criteria. In appropriate cases, Members shall work in cooperation with relevant intergovernmental and non-governmental organisations

towards the establishment and adoption of common international standards and criteria for recognition and common international standards for the practice of relevant services trades and professions.

PART III
SPECIFIC COMMITMENTS

Article XVI
Market Access

1. With respect to market access through the modes of supply identified in Article I, each Member shall accord services and service suppliers of any other Member treatment no less favourable than that provided for under the terms, limitations and conditions agreed and specified in its Schedule.[8]

2. In sectors where market-access commitments are undertaken, the measures which a Member shall not maintain or adopt either on the basis of a regional subdivision or on the basis of its entire territory, unless otherwise specified in its Schedule, are defined as:
   (a) limitations on the number of service suppliers whether in the form of numerical quotas, monopolies, exclusive service suppliers or the requirements of an economic needs test;[9]
   (b) limitations on the total value of service transactions or assets in the form of numerical quotas or the requirement of an economic needs test;

---

[8] If a Member undertakes a market-access commitment in relation to the supply of a service through the mode of supply referred to in subparagraph 2(a) of Article I and if the cross-border movement of capital is an essential part of the service itself, that Member is thereby committed to allow such movement of capital. If a Member undertakes a market-access commitment in relation to the supply of a service through the mode of supply referred to in subparagraph 2(c) of Article I, it is thereby committed to allow related transfers of capital into its territory.

[9] Subparagraph 2(c) does not cover measures of a Member which limit inputs for the supply of services.

(c) limitations on the total number of service operations or on the total quality of service output expressed in terms of designated numerical units in the form of quotas or the requirement of an economic needs test;

(e) measures which restrict or require specific types of legal entity or joint venture through which a service supplier may supply a service; and

(f) limitations on the participation of foreign capital in terms of maximum percentage limit on foreign shareholding or the total value of individual or aggregate foreign investment.

Article XVII
National Treatment

1. In the sectors inscribed in its Schedule, and subject to any conditions and qualifications set out therein, each Member shall accord to services and service suppliers of any other Member, in respect of all measures affecting the supply of services, treatment no less favourable than that it accords to its own like services and service suppliers.[10]

2. A Member may meet the requirement of paragraph 1 by according to services and service suppliers of any other Member, either formally identical treatment or formally different treatment to that it accords to its own like services and service suppliers.

3. Formally identical or formally different treatment shall be considered to be less favourable if it modifies the conditions of competition in favour of services or service suppliers of the Member compared to like services or service suppliers of any other Member.

---

[10] Specific commitments assumed under this Article shall not be construed to require any Member to compensate for any inherent competitive disadvantages which result from the foreign character of the relevant services or service suppliers.

Article XVIII
Additional Commitments

Members may negotiate commitments with respect to measures affecting trade in services not subject to scheduling under Articles XVI or XVII, including those regarding qualifications, standards or licensing matters. Such commitments shall be inscribed in a Member's Schedule.

PART IV
PROGRESSIVE LIBERALISATION

Article XIX
Negotiation of Specific Commitments

1. In pursuance of the objectives of this Agreement, Members shall enter into successive rounds of negotiations, beginning not later than five years from the date of entry into force of the WTO Agreement and periodically thereafter, with a view to achieving a progressively higher level of liberalisation. Such negotiations shall be directed to the reduction or elimination of the adverse effects on trade in services of measures as a means of providing effective market access. This process shall take place with a view to promoting the interests of all participants on a mutually advantageous basis and to securing an overall balance of rights and obligations.

2. The process of liberalisation shall take place with due respect for national policy objectives and the level of development of individual Members, both overall and in individual sectors. There shall be appropriate flexibility for individual developing country Members for opening fewer sectors, liberalising fewer types of transactions, progressively extending market access in line with their development situation and, when making access to their markets available to foreign service suppliers, attaching to such access conditions aimed at achieving the objectives referred to in Article IV.

3. For each round, negotiating guidelines and procedures shall be established. For the purposes of establishing such guidelines, the Council for Trade in Services shall carry out an assessment of trade in services in overall terms and on a sectoral basis with reference to the objectives of this Agreement, including those set out in paragraph 1 of Article IV. Negotiating guidelines shall establish modalities for the treatment of liberalisation undertaken autonomously by Members since previous negotiations, as well as for the special treatment for least-developed country Members under the provisions of paragraph 3 of Article IV.

4. The process of progressive liberalisation shall be advanced in each such round through bilateral, plurilateral or multilateral negotiations directed towards increasing the general level of specific commitments undertaken by Members under this Agreement.

Article XX
Schedules of Specific Commitments

1. Each Member shall set out in a schedule the specific commitments it undertakes under Part III of this Agreement. With respect to sectors where such commitments are undertaken, each Schedule shall specify:

   (a) terms, limitations and conditions on market access;
   (b) conditions and qualifications on national treatment;
   (c) undertakings relating to additional commitments;
   (d) where appropriate the time-frame for implementation of such commitments; and
   (e) the date of entry into force of such commitments.

2. Measures inconsistent with both Articles XVI and XVII shall be inscribed in the column relating to Article XVI. In this case the inscription will be considered to provide a condition or qualification to Article XVII as well.

3. Schedules of specific commitments shall be annexed to this Agreement and shall form an integral part thereof.

Article XXI
Modification of Schedules

1. (a) A Member (referred to in this Article as the "modifying Member") may modify or withdraw any commitment in its Schedule, at any time after three years have elapsed from the date on which that commitment entered into force, in accordance with the provisions of this Article.

   (b) A modifying Member shall notify its intent to modify or withdraw a commitment pursuant to this Article to the Council for Trade in Services no later than three months before the intended date of implementation for the modification or withdrawal.

2. (a) At the request of any Member the benefits of which under this Agreement may be affected (referred to in this Article as an "affected Member") by a proposed modification or withdrawal notified under subparagraph 1(b), the modifying Member shall enter into negotiations with a view to reaching agreement on any necessary compensatory adjustment. In such negotiations and agreement, the Members concerned shall endeavour to maintain a general level of mutually advantageous commitments not less favourable to trade than that provided for in Schedules of specific commitments prior to such negotiations.

   (b) Compensatory adjustments shall be made on a most-favoured-nation basis.

3. (a) If agreement is not reached between the modifying Member and any affected Member before the end of the period provided for negotiations, such affected Member may refer the matter to arbitration. Any affected Member that wishes to enforce a right that it may have to compensation must participate in the arbitration.

   (b) If no affected Member has requested arbitration, the modifying Member shall be free to implement the proposed modification or withdrawal.

4. (a) The modifying Member may not modify or withdraw its commitment until it has made compensatory adjustments in conformity with the findings of the arbitration.

   (b) If the modifying Member implements its proposed modifications or withdrawal and does not comply with the findings of the arbitration, any affected Member that participated in the arbitration may modify or withdraw substantially equivalent benefits in conformity with those findings. Notwithstanding Article II, such a modification or withdrawal may be implemented solely with respect to the modifying Member.

5. The Council for Trade in Services shall establish procedures for ratification or modification of Schedules. Any Member which has modified or withdrawn scheduled commitments under this Article shall modify its Schedule according to such procedures.

ANNEX ON ARTICLE II EXEMPTIONS

Scope

1. This Annex specifies the conditions under which a Member, at the entry into force of this Agreement, is exempted from its obligations under paragraph 1 of Article II.

2. Any new exemptions applied for after the date of entry into force of the WTO Agreement shall be dealt with under paragraph 3 of Article IX of that Agreement.

Review

3. The Council for Trade in Services shall review all exemptions granted for a period of more than 5 years. The first such review shall take place no more than 5 years after the entry into force of the WTO Agreement.

4. The Council for Trade in Services in a review shall:
   (a) examine whether the conditions which created the need for the exemption still prevail; and
   (b) determine the date of any further review.

Termination

5. The exemption of a Member from its obligations under paragraph 1 of Article II of the Agreement with respect to a particular measure terminates on the date provided for in the exemption.

6. In principle, such exemptions should not exceed a period of 10 years. In any event, they shall be subject to negotiation in subsequent trade liberalising rounds.

7. A Member shall notify the Council for Trade in Services at the termination of the exemption period that the inconsistent measure has been brought into conformity with paragraph 1 of Article II.

Lists of Article II Exemptions

[The agreed lists of exemptions under paragraph 2 of Article II will be annexed here in the treaty copy of the WTO Agreement.]

Appendix IV
Annex on Financial Services
(HMSO Misc. No. 28 (1994) (Cm. 2556).

1. Scope and Definition

(a) This Annex applies to measures affecting the supply of financial services. Reference to the supply of a financial service in this Annex shall mean the supply of a service as defined in paragraph 2 of Article I of the Agreement.

(b) For the purposes of subparagraph 3(b) of Article I of the Agreement, "services supplied in the exercise of governmental authority" means the following:
   (i)   activities conducted by a central bank or monetary authority or by any other public entity in pursuit of monetary or exchange rate policies;
   (ii) activities forming part of a statutory system of social security or public retirement plans; and
   (iii) other activities conducted by a public entity for the account or with the guarantee or using the financial resources of the Government.

(c) For the purposes of subparagraph 3(b) of Article I of the Agreement, if a Member allows any of the activities referred to in subparagraphs (b)(ii) or (b)(iii) of this paragraph to be conducted by its financial service suppliers in competition with a public entity or a financial service supplier, "services" shall include such activities.

(d) Subparagraph 3(c) of Article I of the Agreement shall not apply to services covered by this Annex.

2. Domestic Regulation

(a) Notwithstanding any other provisions of the Agreement, a Member shall not be prevented from taking measures for prudential reasons, including for the protection of investors, depositors, policy holders or persons to whom a fiduciary duty is owed by a financial service supplier, or to ensure the integrity and stability of the financial system. Where such measures do not conform with the provisions of the Agreement, they shall not be used as a means of avoiding the member's commitments or obligations under the Agreement.

(b) Nothing in the Agreement shall be construed to require a Member to disclose information relating to the affairs and accounts of individual customers or any confidential or proprietary information in the possession of public entities.

3. Recognition

(a) A Member may recognise prudential measures of any other country in determining how the Member's measures relating to financial services shall be applied. Such recognition, which may be achieved through harmonisation or otherwise, may be based upon an agreement or arrangement with the country concerned or may be accorded autonomously.

(b) A Member that is a party to such an agreement or arrangement referred to in subparagraph (a), whether future or existing, shall afford adequate opportunity for other interested Members to negotiate their accession to such agreements or arrangements, or to negotiate comparable ones with it, under circumstances in which there would be equivalent regulation, oversight, implementation of such regulation, and, if appropriate, procedures concerning the sharing of information between the parties to the agreement or arrangement. Where a Member accords recognition autonomously, it shall afford adequate opportunity for any other Member to demonstrate that such circumstances exist.

(c) Where a Member is contemplating according recognition to prudential measures of any other country, paragraph 4(b) of Article VII shall not apply.

4. Dispute Settlement

Panels for disputes on prudential issues and other financial matters shall have the necessary expertise relevant to the specific financial services under dispute.

5. Definitions

For the purposes of this Annex:
(a) A financial service is any service of a financial nature offered by a financial service supplier of a Member. Financial services include all insurance and insurance-related services, and all banking and other financial services (excluding insurance). Financial services include the following activities:

Insurance and insurance-related services
(i)   Direct insurance (including co-insurance):
        (A) life
        (B) non-life
(ii)   Reinsurance and retrocession;
(iii)   Insurance intermediation, such as brokerage and agency;
(iv)   Services auxiliary to insurance, such as consultancy, actuarial, risk assessment and claim settlement services.

Banking and other financial services (excluding insurance)
(v)   Acceptance of deposits and other repayable funds from the public;
(vi)   Lending of all types, including consumer credit, mortgage credit, factoring and financing of commercial transactions;
(vii)   Financial leasing;
(viii) All payment and money transmission services, including credit, charge and debit cards, travellers cheques and bankers drafts;
(ix)   Guarantees and commitments;
(x)   Trading for own account or for account of customers, whether on an exchange, in an over-the-counter market or otherwise, the following:

(A) money market instruments (including cheques, bills, certificates of deposits);

(B) foreign exchange;

(C) derivative products including, but not limited to, futures and options;

(D) exchange rate and interest rate instruments, including products such as swaps, forward rate agreements;

(E) transferable securities;

(F) other negotiable instruments and financial assets, including bullion.

(xi) Participation in issues of all kinds of securities, including underwriting and placement as agent (whether publicly or privately) and provision of services related to such issues;

(xii) Money broking;

(xiii) Asset management, such as cash or portfolio management, all forms of collective investment management, pension fund management, custodial, depository and trust services;

(xiv) Settlement and clearing services for financial assets, including securities, derivative products, and other negotiable instruments;

(xv) Provision and transfer of financial information, and financial data processing and related software by suppliers of other financial services;

(xvi) Advisory, intermediation and other auxiliary financial services on all the activities listed in subparagraphs (v) through (xv), including credit reference and analysis, investment and portfolio research and advice, advice on acquisitions and on corporate restructuring and strategy.

(b) A financial service supplier means any natural or juridical person of a Member wishing to supply or supplying financial services but the term "financial service supplier" does not include a public entity.

(c) "Public entity" means:
- (i)   a government, a central bank or a monetary authority, of a Member, or an entity owned or controlled by a Member, that is principally engaged in carrying out governmental functions or activities for governmental purposes, not including an entity principally engaged in supplying financial services on commercial terms; or
- (ii)   a private entity, performing functions normally performed by a central bank or monetary authority, when exercising those functions.

SECOND ANNEX ON FINANCIAL SERVICES (HMSO Misc. 28(1994) (Cm.2556)).

1. Notwithstanding Article II of the Agreement and paragraphs 1 and 2 of the Annex on Article II Exemptions, a Member may, during a period of 60 days beginning four months after the date of entry into force of the WTO Agreement, list in that Annex measures relating to financial services which are inconsistent with paragraph 1 of Article II of the Agreement.

2. Notwithstanding Article XXI of the Agreement, a Member may, during a period of 60 days beginning four months after the date of entry into force of the WTO Agreement, improve, modify or withdraw all or part of the specific commitments on financial services inscribed in its Schedule.

3. The Council for Trade in Services shall establish any procedures necessary for the application of paragraphs 1 and 2.

UNDERSTANDING ON COMMITMENTS IN FINANCIAL SERVICES (HMSO. Misc. No14 (1994) (Cm. 2570)

Participants in the Uruguay Round have been enabled to take on specific commitments with respect to financial services under the General Agreement on Trade in Services (hereinafter referred to as the "Agreement") on the basis of an alternative approach to that covered by the provisions of Part III of the Agreement. It was agreed that this approach could be applied subject to the following understanding:

(i)   it does not conflict with the provisions of the Agreement;

(ii)   it does not prejudice the right of any Member to schedule its specific commitments in accordance with the approach under part III of the Agreement;

(iii)   resulting specific commitments shall apply on a most-favoured-nation basis;

(iv)   no presumption has been created as to the degree of liberalisation to which a Member is committing itself under the Agreement.

Interested Members, on the basis of negotiations, and subject to conditions and qualifications where specified, have inscribed in their schedule specific commitments conforming to the approach set out below.

A. Standstill

Any conditions, limitations and qualifications to the commitments noted below shall be limited to existing non-conforming measures.

B. Market Access.

Monopoly Rights

1. In addition to Article VIII of the Agreement, the following shall apply:

Each Member shall list in its schedule pertaining to financial services existing monopoly rights and shall endeavour to eliminate them or reduce their scope. Notwithstanding subparagraph 1(b) of the Annex on Financial Services, this paragraph applies to the activities referred to in subparagraph 1(b)(iii) of the Annex.

Financial Services purchased by Public Entities

2. Notwithstanding Article XIII of the Agreement, each Member shall ensure that financial service suppliers of any other Member established in its territory are accorded most-favoured-nation treatment and national treatment as regards the purchase or acquisition of financial services by public entities of the member in its territory.

Cross-border Trade

3. Each Member shall permit non-resident suppliers of financial services to supply, as a principal, through an intermediary or as an intermediary, and under terms and conditions that accord national treatment, the following services;

   (a) insurance of risks relating to:
       (i) maritime shipping and commercial aviation and space launching and freight (including satellites), with such insurance to cover any or all of the following: the goods being transported, the vehicle transporting the goods and any liability arising therefrom; and
       (ii) goods in international transit;

   (b) reinsurance and retrocession and the services auxiliary to insurance as referred to in subparagraph 5(a)(iv) of the Annex;

   (c) provision and transfer of financial information and financial data processing as referred to in subparagraph 5(a)(xv) of the Annex and advisory and other auxiliary services, excluding intermediation, relating to banking and other financial services as referred to in subparagraph 5(a)(xvi) of the Annex.

4. Each Member shall permit its residents to purchase in the territory of any other Member the financial services indicated in:

(a) subparagraph 3(a);
(b) subparagraph 3(b); and
(c) subparagraphs 5(a)(v) to (xvi) of the Annex.

Commercial Presence
5. Each Members shall grant financial service suppliers of any other member the right to establish or expand within its territory, including through the acquisition of existing enterprises, a commercial presence.

6. A Member may impose terms, conditions and procedures for authorisation of the establishment and expansion of a commercial presence in so far as they do not circumvent the member's obligation under paragraph 5 and they are consistent with the other obligations of the Agreement.

New Financial Services
7. A Member shall permit financial service suppliers of any other Member established in its territory to offer in its territory any new financial services.

Transfers of Information and Processing of Information
8. No Member shall take measures that prevent transfers of information or the processing of financial information, including transfers of data by electronic means, or that, subject to importation rules consistent with international agreements, prevent transfers of equipment, where such transfers of information processing of financial information or transfers of equipment are necessary for the conduct of the ordinary business of a financial service supplier. Nothing in this paragraph restricts the right of a member to protect personal data, personal privacy and the confidentiality of individual records and accounts so long as such right is not used to circumvent the provisions of the Agreement.

Temporary Entry of Personnel

9.   (a) Each Member shall permit temporary entry into its territory of the following personnel of a financial service supplier of any other Member that is establishing or has established a commercial presence in the territory of the member:

(i) senior managerial personnel possessing proprietary information essential to the establishment, control and operation of the services of the financial service supplier; and

(ii) specialists in the operation of the financial service supplier.

    (b) Each Member shall permit, subject to the availability of qualified personnel in its territory, temporary entry into its territory of the following personnel associated with a commercial presence of a financial service supplier of any other Member;

(i) specialists in computer services, telecommunication services and accounts of the financial service supplier; and

(ii) actuarial and legal specialists.

Non-discriminatory Measures

10.   Each Member shall endeavour to remove or to limit any significant adverse effects on financial service suppliers of any other Member of:

    (a) non-discriminatory measures that prevent financial service suppliers from offering in the Member's territory, in the form determined by the Member, all the financial services permitted by the Member;

    (b) non-discriminatory measures that limit the expansion of the activities of financial service suppliers into the entire territory of the Member;

    (c) measures of a Member, when such a Member applies the same measures to the supply of both banking and securities services, and a financial service supplier of any other Member concentrates its activities in the provision of securities services; and

(d) other measures that, although respecting the provisions of the Agreement, affect adversely the ability of financial service suppliers of any other Member to operate, complete or enter the Member's market;

provided that any action taken under this paragraph would not unfairly discriminate against financial service suppliers of the member taking such action.

11.   With respect to the non-discriminatory measures referred to in subparagraphs 10(a) and (b), a Member shall endeavour not to limit or restrict the present degree of market opportunities nor the benefits already enjoyed by financial service suppliers of all other Members as a class in the territory of the member, provided that this commitment does not result in unfair discrimination against financial service suppliers of the Member applying such measures.

C. National Treatment

1.   Under terms and conditions that accord national treatment, each Member shall grant to financial service suppliers of any other Member established in its territory access to payment and clearing systems operated by public entities, and to official funding and refinancing facilities available in the normal course of ordinary business. This paragraph is not intended to confer access to the Member's lender of last resort facilities.

2.   When membership or participation in, or access to, any self-regulatory body, securities or futures exchange or market, clearing agency, or any other organisation or association, is required by a Member in order for financial service suppliers of any other member to supply financial services on an equal basis with financial service suppliers of the Member, or when the Member provides directly or indirectly such entities, privileges or advantages in supplying financial services, the Member shall ensure that such entities accord national treatment to financial service suppliers of any other Member resident in the territory of the Member.

D. Definitions

For the purposes of this approach:

1. A non-resident supplier of financial services is a financial service supplier of a member which supplies a financial service into the territory of another Member from an establishment located in the territory of another Member, regardless of whether such a financial service supplier has or has not a commercial presence in the territory of the Member in which the financial service is supplied.

2. "Commercial presence" means an enterprise within a Member's territory for the supply of financial services and includes wholly- or partly-owned subsidiaries, joint ventures, partnerships, sole proprietorships, franchising operations, branches, agencies, representative offices or other organisations.

3. A new financial service is a service of a financial nature, including services related to existing and new products or the manner in which a product is delivered, that is not supplied by any financial service supplier in the territory of a particular member but which is supplied in the territory of another Member.

Appendix V

Libraries Holding Copies of Market Access Schedules

Details of individual market access schedules for both goods and services are available at the government libraries listed below. Schedules can be consulted there by appointment and copies of individual schedules and sections of schedules may be ordered by telephone from the DTI Victoria Street Library and Information Centre at the number listed below. A fee will be charged to cover the costs of this service.

Department of Trade & Industry
Victoria Street Library and Information Centre
Ashdown House
123 Victoria Street
London SW1E 6RB
Telephone (0171) 215 4245/4250
Fax (0171) 215 5665

Business Information Library
Industrial Development Board for Northern Ireland
IDB House
64 Chichester Street
Belfast BT4 2JP
Telephone (01232) 233233
Fax (01232) 230653

Scottish Trade International
Scottish Office
120 Bothwell Street
Glasgow G2 7JP
Telephone (0141) 228 2843
Fax (0141) 221 3712

Welsh Office Library
The Welsh Office
New Crown Buildings
Cathays Park
Cardiff CF1 3NQ
Telephone (01222) 825449/823683
Fax (01222) 823036

Appendix VI
Working Procedures of DSB Panels
(HMSO Misc. No. 15 (1994) (Cm. 2571))

1. In its proceedings the panel shall follow the relevant provisions of this Understanding. In addition, the following working procedures shall apply.

2. The panel shall meet in closed session. The parties to the dispute, and interested parties, shall be present at the meetings only when invited by the panel to appear before it.

3. The deliberations of the panel and the documents submitted to it shall be kept confidential. Nothing in this Understanding shall preclude a party to a dispute from disclosing statements of its own positions to the public. Members shall treat as confidential information submitted by another Member to the panel which that member has designated as confidential. Where a party to a dispute submits a confidential version of its written submissions to the panel, it shall also, upon request of a Member, provide a non-confidential summary of the information contained in its submissions that could be disclosed to the public.

4. Before the first substantive meeting of the panel with the parties, the parties to the dispute shall transmit to the panel written submissions in which they present the facts of the case and their arguments.

5. At its first substantive meeting with the parties, the panel shall ask the party which has brought the complaint to present its case. Subsequently, and still at the same meeting, the party against which the complaint has been brought shall be asked to present its point of view.

6. All third parties which have notified their interest in the dispute to the DBS shall be invited in writing to present their views during a session of the first substantive meeting of the panel set aside for that purpose. All such third parties may be present during the entirety of this session.

7. Formal rebuttals shall be made at a second substantive meeting of the panel. The party complained against shall have the right to take the floor first to be followed by the complaining party. The parties shall submit, prior to that meeting, written rebuttals to the panel.

8. The panel may at any time put questions to the parties and ask them for explanations either in the course of a meeting with the parties or in writing.

9. The parties to the dispute and any third party invited to present its views in accordance with Article 10 shall make available to the panel a written version of their oral statements.

10.In the interest of full transparency, the presentations, rebuttals and statements referred to in paragraphs 5 to 9 shall be made in the presence of the parties. Moreover, each party's written submissions, including any comments on the descriptive part of the report and responses to questions put by the panel, shall be made available to the other party or parties.

11.Any additional procedures specific to the panel.

12.Proposed timetable for panel work:

    (a) Receipt of first written submissions of the parties:
       (1)Complaining party: - 3-6 weeks
       (2)Party complained against: - 2-3 weeks

    (b)Date, time and place of first substantive meeting with the parties; third party session: - 1-2 weeks

    (c) Receipt of written rebuttals of the parties: - 2-3 weeks

    (d)Date, time and place of second substantive meeting with the parties: - 1-2 weeks

(e) Issuance of descriptive part of the report to the parties: - 2-4 weeks

(f) Receipt of comments by the parties on the descriptive part of the report: - 2 weeks

(g) Issuance of the interim report, including the findings and conclusions, to the parties: - 2-4 weeks

(h) Deadline for party to request review of part(s) of report - 1 week

(i) Period of review by panel, including possible additional meeting with parties: - 2 weeks

(j) Issuance of final report to parties to dispute: - 2 weeks

(k) Circulation of the final report to the Members: - 3 weeks

The above calendar may be changed in the light of unforeseen developments. Additional meetings with the parties shall be scheduled if required.